# FRENCH CURVES

DELAHAYE • DELAGE • TALBOT-LAGO

MULLIN AUTOMOTIVE MUSEUM

DELAHAYE
632

# FRENCH CURVES

## DELAHAYE • DELAGE • TALBOT-LAGO
MULLIN AUTOMOTIVE MUSEUM

Richard Adatto
with Claude Figoni
and Shana Hinds
Photographs by Michael Furman

# TABLE OF CONTENTS

*From left; race car drivers Laury Schell, René Dreyfus and Louis Gérard at Cork, Ireland, 1938.*

# PREFACE:
# DELAHAYE, DELAGE, TALBOT-LAGO

I have dreamed about cars since I was a child, envisioning myself riding in and driving all sorts of beautiful automobiles. I started with GM styling in the 1950s (a Chevy Bel-Air), but was later drawn to the sophisticated coachwork of the foreign cars prevalent in the Los Angeles area (a Porsche 356). As I gained more exposure to quality cars, my tastes came to focus on the creations of the French art deco movement. These works of art, which became my life's passion, are exemplified in the collection of paintings, sculpture, furniture, and automobiles now displayed in The Mullin Automotive Museum.

This is the second volume in a series of books we are publishing to allow people the opportunity to experience the collection and learn about Delahaye, Delage, and Talbot-Lago, as well as the coachbuilders who produced the fantastic bodies for these marques. These cars shaped modern automotive styling, and they are now considered to have been at the design forefront of their era. Prior to the mid-1930s, designers were testing various styling approaches, trying to find a concept that would epitomize modern coachwork. At the 1936 Paris Auto Salon, the Figoni & Falaschi Type 135 Delahaye roadster amalgamated the designs of the period, successfully defining streamlined art deco styling. The years that followed further developed the genre, witnessing the birth of the 1939 Delahaye Type 165 New York World's Fair show car and the Talbot-Lago Type 150-C-SS Teardrop. These are the cars that make up the heart of my collection. They are three of my favorite cars, just as accounts tell us that they were the favorites of coachbuilder Joseph Figoni, who created the styling on all three. Figoni's design inspiration came from the aerodynamic pontoons of a French airplane model, the *Arc-en-Ciel*, that was in his office—and the rest is history!

– Peter Mullin
Chairman, Mullin Automotive Museum
August 2011

Julien Philippy

# FOREWORD:
# THOUGHTS ON A MASTER COACHBUILDER

My father, Joseph Figoni, set up his workshop in 1923 at 14 rue Lemoine in Boulogne sur Seine, a Paris suburb, with his wife, Victorine. At that time, coachwork was considered artisanal in nature, and he had prepared extensively for his calling, beginning an apprenticeship with Parisian carriage maker Émile Vachet at the age of 14. Joseph began his business by modifying existing coachwork, restyling the front and rear fenders on Bugatti, Delage, and other major marques. His fine craftsmanship and styling soon drew notice at the various concours d'élégance. From restyling, Joseph progressed to designing and building complete bodies; his successful 1925 coachwork on Ballot and Bugatti prompted him to have his first stand at the 1929 Paris Auto Salon, where he featured his work on a Bugatti.

During the early days of the company there were many orders for cars. Between 1925 and 1935, this small firm built about 300 bodies: 75 on Bugatti, 84 on Delage, 27 on Alfa, 19 on Ford, 20 on Hotchkiss, and 65 on Ballot. But despite Joseph's popularity as a coachbuilder, the size of the company meant that they were often operating with finances in the red. Joseph Figoni was an artist, but definitely not an expert in economics. In 1935, he solved the problem by making Ovidio Falaschi, a Tuscan entrepreneur, a partner in the firm, which became Figoni & Falaschi. Falaschi was able to handle the business side of the company, signing contracts and ensuring cash flow, which freed up Joseph to focus on his creations and truly express his talents.

Joseph Figoni's inspirations came primarily from the many aspects of nature, everything from birds and fish to flowers and women. Always striving for harmonious lines and fluidity between a car's body and wings,

*Joseph Figoni and his wife, Victorine, with Claude Figoni and his wife, Eliane, drinking champagne together in 1961.*

*The pontoon fenders on the* Arc-en-Ciel *plane were one of the inspirations for the fenders of the 1936 Paris Auto Salon Type 135.*

Joseph would spend hours devising and revising the grand plan of a model. A design was always a big success or a total disaster, because it was hard to set the first reference point, to locate the body precisely on the chassis according to the car manufacture's plan and ideas, and then to shape that body. Joseph was also inspired by aviation, especially Couzinet's plane, the *Arc-en-Ciel* ("Rainbow"). The pontoon covers of the plane's landing gear gave my father his inspiration for the wings of the 1936 Paris Auto Salon Delahaye, a car that proved to be the seminal design of a new international movement in car styling.

My father was lucky to work with a great Swiss designer, Amédée Mermoz, who was very talented at producing full-size drawings of cars. I stayed with Amédée and his mother at their home in Switzerland and came to know him very well. As a boy, I was with both him and my father as they developed the 1936 Paris Auto Salon Delahaye.

Thanks to his avant-garde lines and aerodynamic style, Joseph became more and more famous. By 1936 he was working with Delahaye and Talbot-Lago a great deal, having established himself as a famous coachbuilder. These manufacturers were seduced by the Figoni outlines, and strong collaborations took place between marque and coachbuilder. At the 1937 Paris Auto Salon, the Figoni stand featured the Talbot-Lago Type 150-C-SS Aerodynamic Coupé, which the press dubbed the *Goutte d'Eau* ("Teardrop"). The model's styling was a media sensation and is still considered the most classic of French automotive designs.

Joseph's approach to construction was hands-on. He would start with a simple sketch, then refine the drawing. Sometimes he would hone the design further by sculpting a clay likeness, often making a scale model carved from wood. For the next step, metal workers would reproduce a full-size representation, bending thin metal strips into the contours of the design and fastening them to the chassis to create a mock-up of the body's shape. After client approval was received, my father would have a draftsman make a full-size drawing, called the grand plan, from which the car was built. The carpenters would construct a wood-framed shell that would be fixed to the chassis. Panel-beating started next: steel or aluminum for both the shell of the body and the very intricate work of the wings, which would take days. Next, the manufacturer's signature grill or a custom, Figoni-designed badge was placed on the chassis, then the rest of the metalwork could be performed and the doors set. After the body was complete, they used lead filler to make it all smooth before sending the car to be painted. The process of choosing a color was exceedingly tedious for the painter, because my father always wanted a shade inspired by a flower, a piece of fabric, or a painting, which took time. Lastly came the finishing touches: wood trim on the doors and dashboard, chrome plating on the body and finally, leather work on the upholstery.

After meeting Joseph Figoni at a salon or concours d'élégance, a customer could either instantly place an order for a model featured at the event, or make an appointment to see various models at the workshop. Sometimes, a customer would order at a marque's stand, buy the chassis, and then choose a coachbuilder. My father would often design an exclusive body with several unique details for each customer, but he also frequently imposed his choices on the customers. Joseph was always available to his clients, helping them to visit his workshop and showing them those bodies in the works. After the 1936 and 1937 Paris Auto Salons, there was a great deal of mail, from both France and abroad, asking for quotes and pictures of a given model. In addition to all the publicity it received at the salons and concours d'élégance, the company also advertised in luxury magazines.

World War II postponed coachbuilding for Figoni & Falaschi. The workshop was requisitioned by the French government to make aircraft components for the war effort. During the German occupation, my father left Paris for the Dordogne, a region in the southwest of France, but was brought back to make household appliances like stoves and refrigerators. The German government forced Joseph and his staff to work on the prototype wings of a new secret jet fighter project,

*Figoni & Falaschi put its coachbuilder badge on every car on both sides of the body work, usually below the doors.*
*Following pages: Patent drawing depicting Figoni's "enveloppantes" – the fully-enveloped pontoon fenders.*

although they were not told what they were building. The best craftsmen were put on the job, working slowly and carefully and always purposely introducing small miscalculations. As a result, the wings never became a viable reality. This "failure" caused some trouble for my father and his men, but fortunately the war ended before the Germans could bring too much pressure to bear.

After the war, new industrial regulations and tax laws gradually doomed the French coachbuilding industry. Ovidio Falaschi returned to Italy, where he purchased a hotel at Marina Massa. General Motors tried to hire my father to come to America and work as a designer, but he was unwilling to leave his family and clients.

He eventually retired, and I took over the workshop with my father as my mentor. We continued to produce custom coachwork as long as Delahaye and the other marques were in business. Those were our most profitable years, with the greatest part of our money coming from American orders. Joseph's last work was in 1952 on a Delahaye Type 235 and on sixteen Simca Sports chassis, which he purchased for business that never came. After 1954, there was no longer any call for custom coachwork. My father, Joseph Figoni, passed away in 1978, and the firm continued under my direction as a Lancia dealer until 1989, at which time it joined the other French coachbuilders of the past.

Gone, but not forgotten, Figoni & Falaschi had a lasting influence on automotive styling. Modern designers still refer to the look and feel of my father's cars for inspiration, and the legacy of his company can be found in the aerodynamic coachwork he placed upon the chassis that characterized the car's Golden Age. That coachwork, with its fluid beauty and speed-inspired curves, was what my father's clients wanted. It was what made them true devotees of not only the automobile, but of the streamlined styling that defined the era. Now, as then, the designs of Joseph Figoni inspire admiration, adoration, and imitation—but never replication.

— Claude Figoni
June 2011

N° 827.640

Société à respon

Établissement

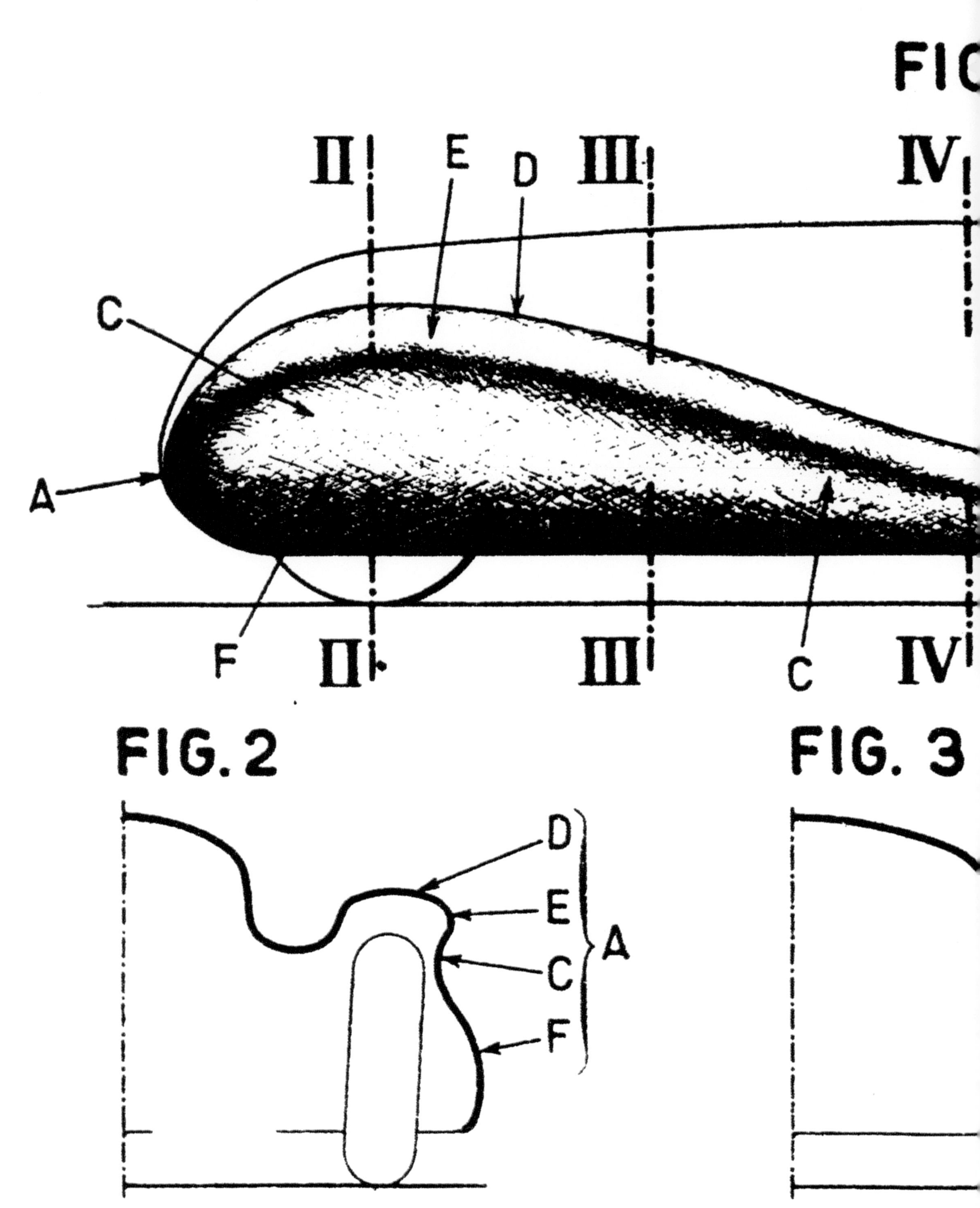

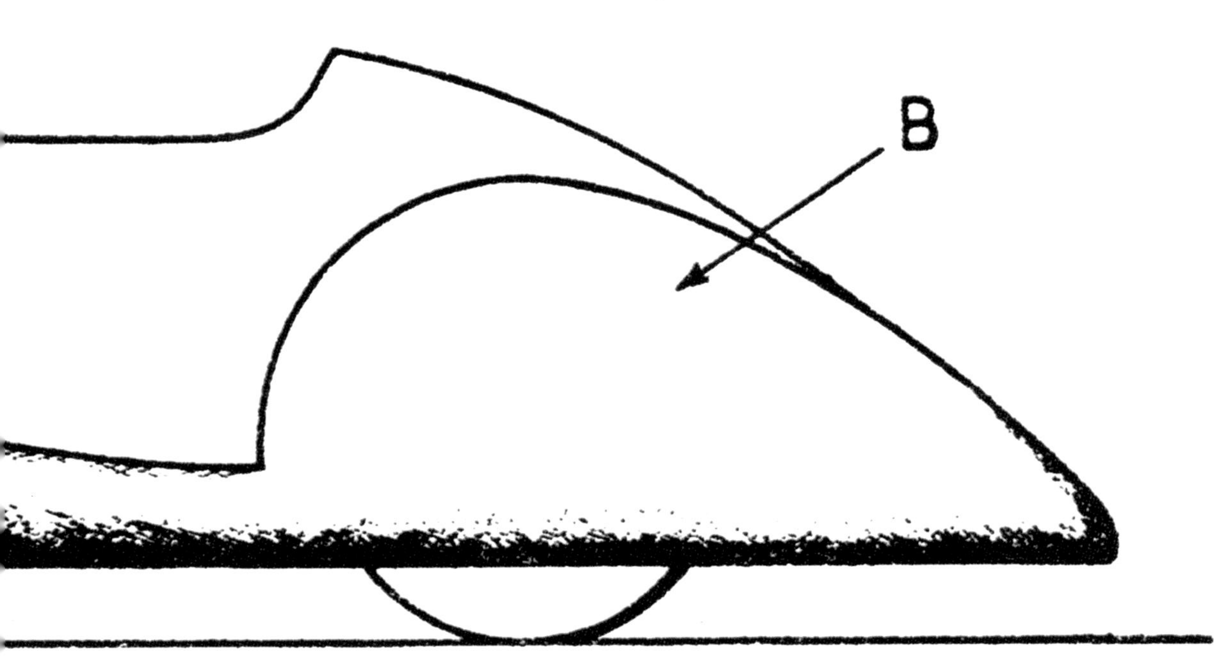


FIG. 4

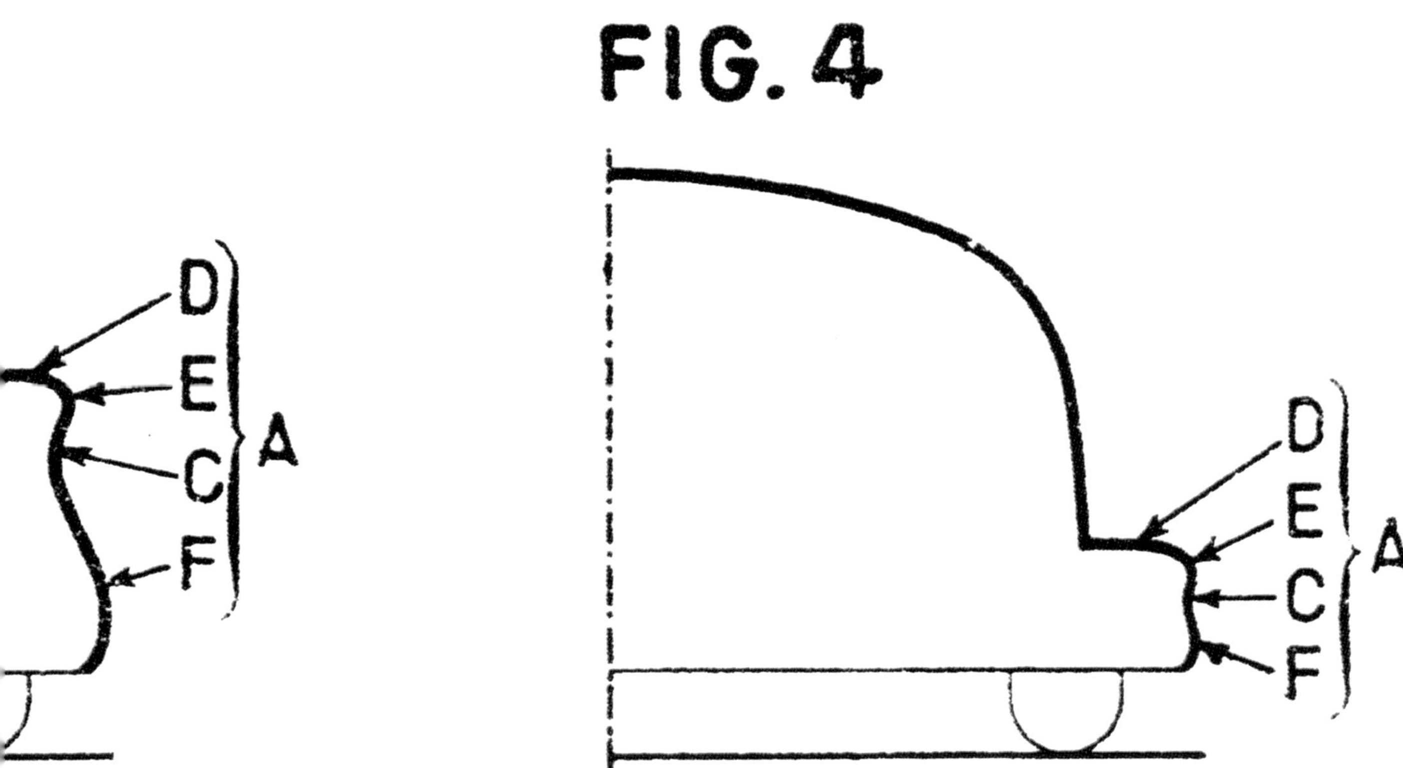

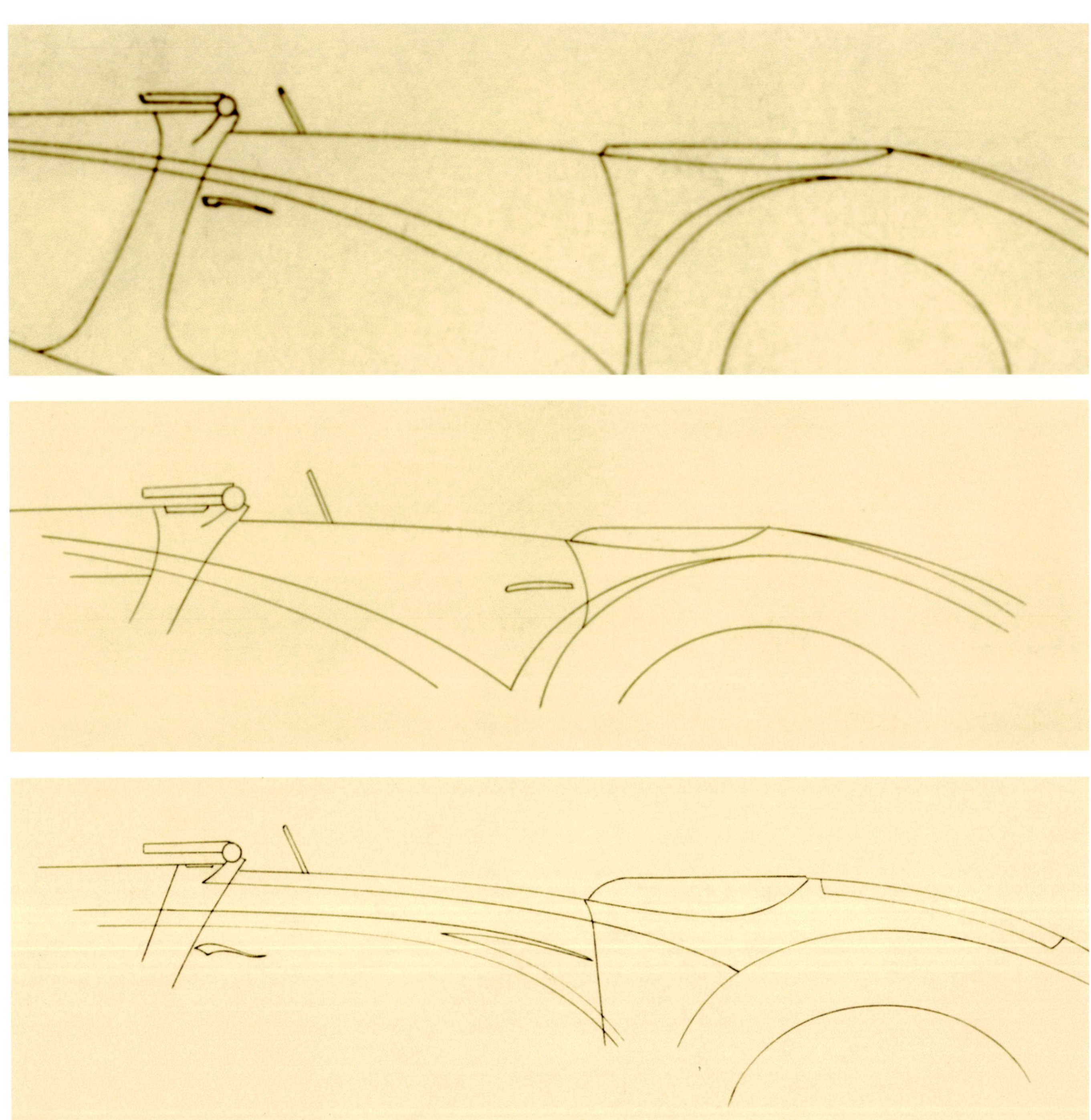

*Various style drawings from the Figoni & Falaschi workshop. Such depictions were used to give customers options and ideas when ordering cars. These drawings were created between 1936 and 1939.*

## CLAUDE FIGONI

From childhood, Claude Figoni was intimately involved in his father's coachbuilding business. He began helping out in the workshop in the late 1930s, assisting the craftsmen and learning the trade from the ground up. After World War II, he attended college in England. Upon graduation, Claude returned to France and resumed his place at his father's workshop, where he was instrumental in the post-war success of Figoni & Falaschi. After Ovidio Falaschi left the company in 1951 (at which time it became Etablissements Figoni & Cie.), Claude took over as director and helped his father run the firm during its most profitable era. In the mid-1950s, by which time custom coachbuilding had become *démodé*, the workshop focused on repair and became a Lancia dealership, which lasted until Claude's retirement in 1989.

*"Ironically, because of the demand for custom coachwork from the United States, we made more money after the war than before, which was unique for French coachbuilders."*
*- Claude Figoni*

# CURATOR'S INTRODUCTION: THE INFLUENCE OF FRENCH DESIGN

What characteristics define and distinguish the classic French automobile, and why has it been so influential? I recently posed this question to a number of automotive designers and received the same answer – passion, romance, innovation. When I pressed them to identify for me the specific formal elements that produce this emotive response they once again all gave me the same answer, which was that it is hard to articulate the precise origin or aspect, but that it is clear when experienced. And perhaps this is why we love French automobiles – their beguiling nature and elusive quality that cannot be named. What is evident from our current vantage point is that French automobiles have captivated and inspired people for generations, wielding influence around the globe in a variety of media. At the Mullin Automotive Museum we perceive the French automobile as a champion of design.

In its first volume, *The Art of Bugatti*, the Mullin Automotive Museum celebrated the manifold creations of a family whose works represent an artistic renaissance spanning the nineteenth and twentieth centuries. For many people, Bugatti defines French automobiles, and yet Ettore was born in Milan, and Molsheim was not always part of France. For many others Delahaye, Delage, and Talbot-Lago are the heart and soul of the French automobile and epitomize French design.

Delahaye, Delage, and Talbot-Lago produced exceptional automobiles and provided an industrial platform upon which artisans transformed an industry from one focused more strictly on the functional aspects of transportation to one that understood the value of artistic investigation, the real benefit of thoughtful and progressive design, and the potential success and delight that it might produce.

– Andrew Reilly
Deputy Director and Chief Curator,
Mullin Automotive Museum
June 2011

AVIONS VOISIN
ESERVE COLLECTION

# DELAHAYE

# A BRIEF HISTORY OF DELAHAYE

*Facing page: Magazine advertisement from the late 1930s. Translation: "Leave! Only a car that is generous, powerful, fast and reliable, with an incomparably pleasant drive, allows you to taste without hesitation the joys of the road. Leave at the wheel of a DELAHAYE. An uninterrupted continuation of sensational victories that haven't stopped proving for years the remarkable value of this stunning car."*

The Delahaye company enjoyed a long history, starting in the early days of the automobile and ending in the middle of the twentieth century, almost six decades later. Its founder, Émile Delahaye, was born on October 16, 1843, in Tours, France, on the banks of the river Loire. He was educated at the École Nationale Supérieure d'Arts et Métiers, a nation-wide network of technical colleges, graduating as a mechanical engineer in 1869. He then worked for several years with a manufacturer of steam engines, railway equipment, and locomotives. This experience was to come in handy when he and his wife purchased a small foundry in his hometown.

Émile began by making innovative 4-stroke internal combustion engines, building up a range of vertical and horizontal power units suitable for motorboats or for generators and pumps. From there, it was only a small step to creating his own car, which he accomplished in 1894 when he was fifty-one years old. The Delahaye company was founded shortly thereafter.

In 1896, to advertise his newly established business, Delahaye decided to enter the Paris-Marseille-Paris race, an arduous contest organized by the Automobile Club of France (ACF). One Delahaye, piloted by Émile himself, placed tenth overall and second in its class. A second Delahaye placed seventh overall and first in its class. This strong performance resulted in early fame and recognition for the marque, but apart from a few unsuccessful subsequent forays, Delahaye did not venture into racing again until many years later.

In 1897, Émile began to look for larger quarters for his prosperous company. He formed a partnership with Georges Morane and Léon Desmarais, both of who contributed the capital Émile needed to move to 10 rue du Banquier in the Gobelin district of Paris. In 1898, the newly created Société Delahaye et Compagnie hired two promising young men: Amédée Varlet, who was to take charge of the design department, and Charles Weiffenbach, who was to be head of production. By that time, Émile was suffering from ill health, and he and his wife soon decided to retire to their home in Vouvray, just east of Tours. They had no children to take their places, so in 1901 they sold the business to Morane and Desmarais, with whom they had become close friends. Even after his departure from the firm, Émile generously continued to share his knowledge and experience with the new owners. He died on June 1, 1905, at the age of sixty-one.

Management was taken over by Weiffenbach, who was from Thann, Alsace, on France's eastern border. Born in 1870, "Monsieur Charles," as he was known with affection and respect, was another impressive product of the Arts et Métiers system. He was to become the driving force at Delahaye throughout the remainder of its history, and he remained true to what was by then its slogan, *Solide comme une Delahaye* ("As solid as a Delahaye"). He made the company's utility vehicle department deservedly famous by expanding it to include trucks, mechanical plows, dinghies, ambulances, road sweepers, mail vans, and hearses. For more than forty years, Delahaye had an almost complete monopoly on French fire trucks and was the first company to equip them with high-volume pumps.

The strong technical achievements of the company came into play during World War I, enabling Delahaye to produce shells, aircraft engines, and most notably its 1914 Type 59 truck. This truck, with a 4-cylinder motor delivering 30 hp, was recognized for its steady and heroic performance during the Battle of Verdun. Delahaye farm equipment also proved reliable and helped to provision France throughout the conflict. By the end of the war, the company was wealthy, respected, and known throughout the world.

After the armistice in 1919, automobile production resumed with only one model, the Type 64-N. But according to Delahaye historian Jacques Rousseau, "by 1924, Delahaye had completed its range of models, a 'classic' spread that remained unchanged until 1928. Sober elegance was the keynote of all Delahayes of this period. Despite the ever-increasing popularity and mechanical excellence of low-priced, mass-produced cars, Delahaye still retained its faithful customers for costly, distinctive cars, an allegiance reminiscent of the early days of the century." By the late 1920s and early 1930s, however, the company had entered a regrettably dull period. "Quality and reliability remained high," says Rousseau, "but the cars looked like dozens of others."

Monsieur Charles decided to gamble and aim for a high-performance image, seeking to capture the luxury market. This decision implied forsaking the profitable business of trucks and other utility vehicles. Weiffenbach hired Jean François, a brilliant young engineer, to focus on the automobiles and transform them from underpowered, unremarkable, and highly priced vehicles into something truly noteworthy.

At the 1933 Paris Auto Salon, Delahaye introduced the first two cars in its Superluxe line: the Type 134, with a 4-cylinder, 12 hp engine, and the Type 138, with a 6-cylinder, 18 hp engine. These models were equipped with independent front suspension (IFS) and large, self-adjusting brakes, both firsts for the industry.

The 1933 Paris Auto Salon also saw the presentation of coachbuilder Joseph Figoni's influential design for the streamlined Delahaye "World Record Car." Figoni's concepts were inspired by the new field of aeronautical design and over the next few years, his coachwork would set the standard in the arena of streamlined styling. He was responsible for the bodies of several noteworthy Delahaye Paris Auto Salon show

*Facing page: Delahaye expanded its production from only cars to include fire trucks, vans, and buses in 1905, and continued until 1939. Post-war, the company made some jeeps, but ceased most commercial production.*

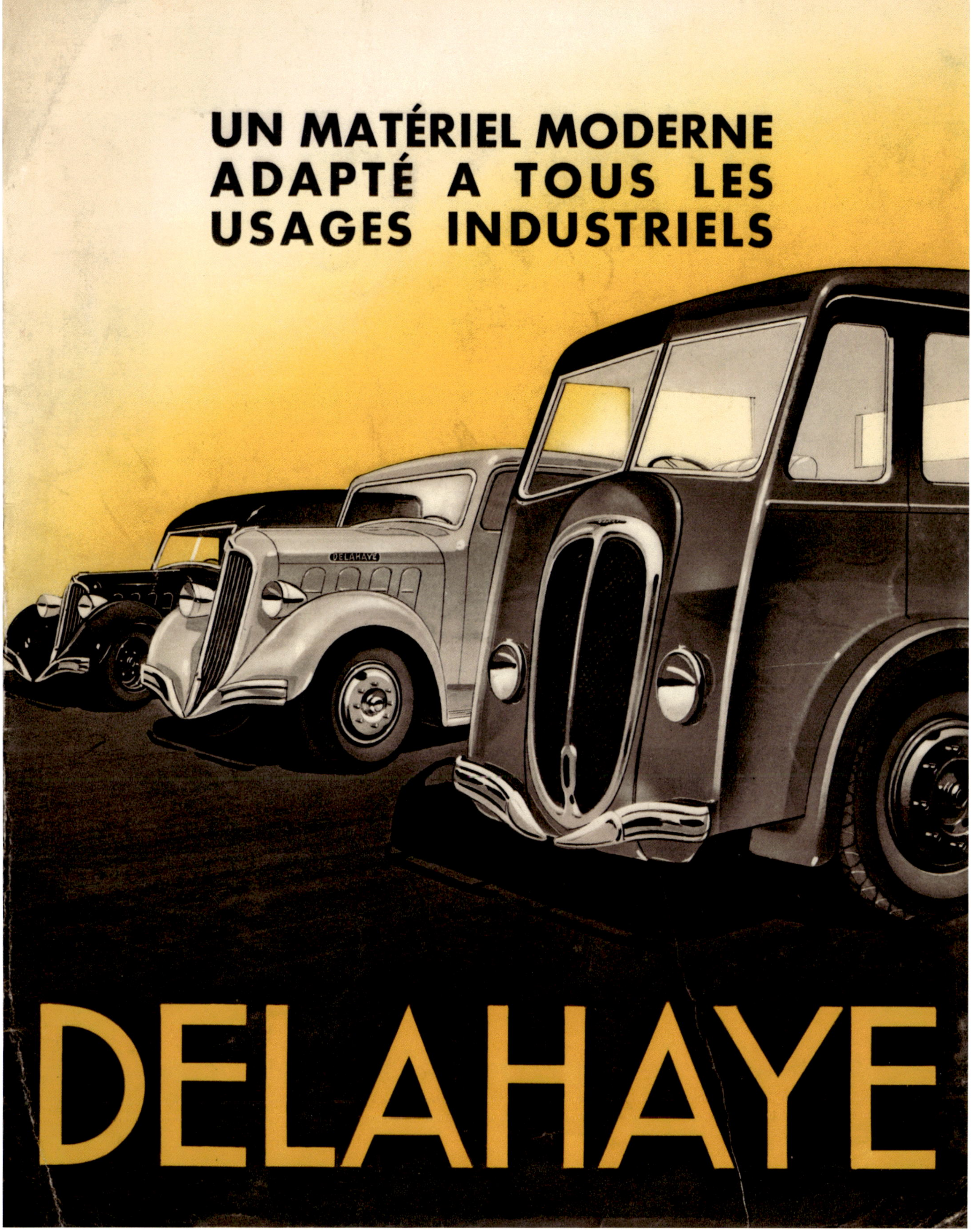

# UN MATÉRIEL MODERNE ADAPTÉ A TOUS LES USAGES INDUSTRIELS



# DELAHAYE

DELAHAYE
PANHARD-LEVASSOR
SORTIE

cars, and his influence on this car was unmistakable: the elliptical shape was repeated front and back with enclosed pontoon fenders; the aerodynamic styling included faired-in headlights, a grill curved to the body's shape, a finned tail, and fine chrome trim; and all four wheels were encased in tapered fenders, called *enveloppantes* by Figoni, which gave the viewer an immediate impression of speed and power.

The Delahaye Type 135 was presented at the Paris Auto Salon of the following year. Compared to the Type 138, which was being produced simultaneously, the new car had a slightly lowered (*surbaissé*) chassis, which lowered its center of gravity and lengthened its line. The Type 135 appeared in a number of incarnations during its first years of production, which were halted abruptly in 1939 by World War II. The first model was the Coupes des Alpes, which was produced from 1935 to 1939. This was followed by the Type 135 Sport (produced from 1935 to 1939); the Type 135 Competition (produced from 1935 to 1938); the Type 135 M Competition (produced in 1938 and 1939); the Type 135 MS (produced in 1938 and 1939); and the Type 135 Competition Court (produced from 1935 to 1939), which had a short chassis and was built in very limited numbers. It is important to note that these models' designations as sport or competition was for marketing purposes. Such titles allowed Delahaye to trade on the activities of its racing cars, which were very successful during this period.

Production resumed in 1946, and the Type 135 M and MS models were produced until 1952, along with the Types 148 and 148 L, which were manufactured from 1936 to 1953. Even in today's faster traffic, the extra horsepower of the Delahaye Type 135 MS engine makes driving this car a great motoring experience.

The touring Type 135s, designed for and used on the road, led gentle lives compared to those of their racing brethren, and many went on to enjoy great success at the fashionable concours d'élégance. "For the amateur," says Delahaye historian Jean-Pierre Bernard, "the 135 was the 'genuine' Delahaye. Many were designed by coachbuilder Henri Chapron and it became one of the best examples of the French Golden Age."

In 1935, the Delahaye company assimilated Delage, a prestigious French chassis manufacturer that had been in financial difficulty for several years. Delage's assets were sold to Delahaye, which continued to produce the Delage marque. Delahaye thus inherited many of Delage's well-heeled clients, who demanded performance plus the ultimate in style and comfort. In the words of automobile historian J.R. Buckley, "And so it was that almost within months of its appearance, the soignée silk-lined cloak of elegance, worn so gracefully by Delage for so long, fell upon the waiting shoulders of the 135 Delahaye."

When World War II began in 1939 and Germany invaded France, all French industry was placed at the service of the Nazi war effort. The years it took the Allies to defeat the Third Reich were long, and when the fighting finally came to an end, France's economy was badly crippled. The lack of resources was felt particularly keenly by the automobile industry. In the case of Delahaye, the wartime death of engineer Jean François posed a creative setback for the company.

*Facing page: October 1, 1936, Paris Auto Salon for the 1937 model year; the Type 135 Paris Show Car sits on the Delahaye stand.*

# DELAHAYE TYPE 135M SPECIFICATION

## ENGINE

| | |
|---|---|
| Cylinders | 6 |
| Bore | 84 mm. |
| Stroke | 107 mm. |
| Cylinder capacity | 3.557 litres |
| No. of bearings | 4 |
| B.H.P. | 130 |
| R.A.C. rating | 27 h.p. |
| Valves | Overhead pushrod |
| Carburettors | 3 Downdraught Solex |
| Lubrication | Forced |
| Ignition | Battery—12 volt |
| Electrical equipment | 12 volt |
| Accumulators | 75 A/hours |

## TRANSMISSION

| | |
|---|---|
| Clutch | Dry, single plate |
| Gearbox | Cotal. 4 silent speeds |
| | Top gear—3·42 / 3rd gear—5·60 |
| | 2nd gear—7·60 / 1st gear—11·82 |
| Gleason back axle | 12/41 |

## CHASSIS

| | |
|---|---|
| Brakes | Bendix Servo, 4 wheel |
| Steering | Worm and nut |
| Suspension | Transverse I.F.S. and semi-elliptic rear |
| Shock Absorbers | Friction |
| Wheels | Wire |
| Tyres | 600 x 17 |
| Track | Front 4 ft. 6 ins. Rear 4 ft. 10 ins. |
| Wheelbase | 9 ft. 7 ins. |
| Overall length of chassis | 13 ft. 2 ins. |
| do. width do. | 5 ft. 5 ins. |
| Weight of chassis | 16 cwt. 78 lbs. |
| Total weight with body | 24 cwt. |
| Lbs. weight per c.c. | 0.93 |
| Ground clearance | 9 ins. |
| Turning circle, right lock | 42 ft. |
| do. do. left lock | 41 ft. |

# PERFORMANCE FIGURES

## SPEED

| | |
|---|---|
| Maximum speed | approx. 105 m.p.h. |
| Flying half mile | 98·7 m.p.h. |
| Cruising speed | 80/85 m.p.h. |
| Speed from rest up Test Hill. Gradient 1 in 5 | 25·33 m.p.h. |

## BRAKES

| | |
|---|---|
| Stopping test from 30 m.p.h. on dry concrete surface | 25 ft. |

## ● ACCELERATION TIMES

| | 10 to 30 | 20 to 40 | 30 to 5 |
|---|---|---|---|
| Top gear | 8·6 secs. | 9·3 secs. | 8·7 sec |
| 3rd gear | 5·2 secs. | 5·5 secs. | 6·0 se |
| 2nd gear | 3·8 secs. | 4·6 secs. | — |
| 1st gear | 3·0 secs. | — | — |

Through the gears—

| | |
|---|---|
| 0 to 30 | 4·5 s |
| 0 to 50 | 9·9 s |
| 0 to 60 | 13·7 |
| 0 to 70 | 19·2 |

## NOTES

● The acceleration figures are worthy of note as the times recorded are outstanding and cannot be bettered by any sports car to-day.

The Independent Front Wheel suspension ensures stability at high speeds even over indifferent road surfaces. excellent road holding quality, combined with foolproof gear changing and the powerful Bendix Servo brakes, a driver of average skill to take full advantage of the car's high performance without undue nerve strain.

Due to the excellent design of the body the absence of wind roar, even at speeds of 90 m.p.h., is noteworthy

*Facing page: Sales information dating from the late 1930s; used by car dealers to promote Delahaye in the United Kingdom and United States.*

This period is recalled by Jean-Pierre Bernard, who wrote that as a result of the scarcities, "the first post-war Delahaye was nothing more than a pre-war chassis finished off with whatever parts could be scrounged up. As for the coachbuilders, they equipped these chassis with bodies similar to those of 1939."

Nevertheless, when the automobile salons were able to resume in 1946, Delahaye was in a prominent position. The two chassis preferred by the best coachbuilders were the Types 135 M and 235, both of which seemed to offer excellent prospects for the company's financial future. The Type 235, with its sporty image and sleek coachwork, was particularly encouraging. However, both models ended up taking a back seat when Delahaye, despite its precarious post-war finances, took a risk and launched its Types 175 (short chassis), 178 (medium chassis), and 180 (a very large and heavy chassis), all of which had been under development before the war began. On paper, these cars looked most attractive, boasting powerful 6-cylinder, 4.5-liter overhead camshaft in-line engines. Other features included Dubonnet front suspension, a De Dion rear axle, Lockheed brakes, left-hand drive, a radio, and a heater. The wide chassis also allowed coachbuilders to create appealing, perfectly proportioned bodies. Unfortunately, those bodies were too heavy and overburdened the chassis: the rear transmission half-shaft sheared and the Dubonnet suspension collapsed. After repeated problems with the cars, clients threatened to sue, and the Delahaye company was forced to buy back the models and reimburse its customers.

As the decade progressed, there came a point when custom coachbuilding was no longer financially feasible: the mass production of the 1940s made competition impossible. Identical automobile components rolled off automated assembly lines at a much lower cost than carefully handcrafted products. Traditional coachbuilders and manufacturers, including Delahaye, failed to understand the need to abandon wooden frames and adopt modern metal-framed bodies. At last, in 1950, Delahaye designed a new model in an effort to save the company from its financial difficulties and the tough post-war economy. Two Delahaye prototypes with new metal-framed bodies were built on the Type 235 chassis, which had originally been conceived in 1946. But it was too late.

"The Type 235 should have been launched in 1947 or 1948," explains Jean-Pierre Bernard. "If that had been the case, perhaps Delahaye might still be a major producer of luxury cars. But it wasn't presented until 1951, and a car that should have been a great success was merely a stopgap in the final downfall of the company."

The Delahaye company could go on no longer. Charles Weiffenbach was eighty-four years old, and his fellow directors were just as elderly and anxious to retire. Paul Richard, president of car manufacturer Hotchkiss et Cie, and Pierre Peigney, president of Delahaye, met to study the possibilities of combining their resources. By July 1954 the shareholders of both companies had approved a merger, and a new Hotchkiss-Delahaye corporation was established with a focus on the manufacture of light trucks and Willys jeeps. The fledgling company was reluctant to disengage too abruptly from the luxury Delahaye marque, so it decided to commission a new 6-cylinder, 20 hp coupé on a Hotchkiss chassis (the Agay) and a cabriolet on a Delahaye Type 235 chassis (the Monceau). Both were bodied by coachbuilder Chapron and appeared at the 1954 Paris Auto Salon together with the Delahaye Type 235s still in stock.

This was to be the last appearance of the grand Delahaye name. Shortly afterward, the group was taken over by Brandt, a French corporation specializing in jeeps and other military vehicles and hardware for the French army, and the venerable marque ceased to exist.

*French Delahaye sales brochure, dating from late 1937, promoting new styling options.*

LAHAYE

*Pour l'Elite...*

# 1925 DELAHAYE TYPE 87

*CHASSIS 24932*

*COACHBUILDER: UNKNOWN*

The Type 87 was first introduced at the Paris Auto Salon of 1921 and was produced until 1926 with limited success. It had a 116.9-in. wheelbase; a 1.8-liter, 4-cylinder in-line motor with a fixed head; side valves; a single carburetor; and a 4-speed manual transmission. The brakes were on the rear wheels only, and the car's 30 bhp gave it a top speed of 50 mph. Although the Type 87 was considered to handle well, the styling was conservative and the design and configuration were seen as obsolete at the time of its release. On top of that, the chassis alone cost 17,300 French francs, which was a pretty hefty price in a French economy recovering from World War I.

The early history of Chassis 24932 is unknown at this time. It has formal limousine coachwork by an unknown coachbuilder; unfortunately the identifying body tags are missing. The car is in remarkably original condition, with a beautiful wool interior and a unique interior division window of curved glass that creates a private backseat for passengers. The car was acquired as part of the Schlumpf Reserve Collection, of which it had been part for more than forty years.

LAHAYE

# 1936 DELAHAYE 135

## *CHASSIS 47247*

## *COACHBUILDER: FIGONI & FALASCHI*

Chassis 47247 was largely responsible for bringing streamlined styling to the attention of the world. The torpedo cabriolet coachwork was shown on the circular Delahaye stand at the Paris Auto Salon on October 1, 1936. It was the first in a series of eleven coachwork examples, six of which are known to exist today. This particular example was one of the three built on a short chassis. Figoni & Falaschi's styling caught the attention of the public and the press, the latter of which declared the aerodynamic modeling to be avant-garde. This car was the talk of the salon, which promoted the fame of the Delahaye company and Joseph Figoni like no other event of the time. The following month, the car was displayed at the Olympia Motor Show in London. According to the November 3, 1936, issue of *Motor Magazine*, which listed the car's original cost as 1,285 British pounds:

> *The combined effect of the sweeping lines and pleasantly conceived curves made the special Delahaye sports coupé one of the most talked-of cars at the Olympia Motor Show. It is probably one of the most effective examples of beaten panel work that has been seen for many years. The car bristles with novel features, the wheels being completely enclosed in streamlined wings and auxiliary lights embodied in the fairing. Tail lamps are to be seen in the extreme tips of the rear wings and an additional lamp comes into operation to light up the step-in, when the doors are opened. The effect was enhanced by the color scheme—orange and cream, to wit... The wide tail sweeps up into a slight fin formation.*

*On the far right, Joseph Figoni and Charles Weiffenbach look at the former's masterpiece on the Delahaye stand in October 1936. Ali Khan purchased the car from the salon floor for 100,000 French francs. Note the hand-written chassis reference number, 47247, in the lower left corner.*

*Top: After Ali Khan purchased the car, he sent it back to Figoni to have it repainted black. Note the mention of Geo Ham on this photograph.* *(See page 43 for further discussion.)*

*Bottom: Chassis 47247 as it exists today, without the coachwork, which was lost or destroyed in the late 1940s.*

During the 1936 Paris Auto Salon, the Delahaye was purchased by Ali Khan, who asked the Figoni workshop to change the original orange and cream to black. Windshield wipers and bumpers were also added while the car was being repainted, as they had been nowhere in evidence at the car's debut.

After belonging to Ali Khan, the history of Chassis 47247 has a few gaps. French registration records show that on May 13, 1939, the car was purchased by a dealer who resold it to Raymond Mareuse, who registered it in France under the number 3261YC2. Jean-Pierre Bernard, a past president of the Delahaye Club, recalls seeing the car in Nice after World War II, at which time it had an open, two-passenger roadster body by Vignale of Italy. The car is believed to have remained in the south of France until the 1970s, when Basil Shandom, an exotic car dealer in New Jersey, purchased Chassis 47247 and had it shipped to the United States. The car was advertised in *Hemming Motor News*; no mention of its early history was made. Collector Jim Hull purchased the car in the early 1980s and disliking the Vignale coachwork, had it removed. He then shipped the car's chassis to Los Angeles, where it became part of the Mullin Collection in the mid 1990s. While Mr. Mullin was in the process of buying the car, this author discovered that the engine number matched that of the legendary missing 1936 Paris Auto Salon car. Chassis 47247 is still a rolling chassis with matching numbers, waiting its turn for the restoration it so richly deserves.

*Above: The engine plate of this car matches the chassis number of the Paris Auto Salon car.*

*Interior of the car after being repainted black at the Figoni workshop. Note the Geo Ham credit per the temporary court settlement.* *(See page 43 for further discussion.)*

Création : Figoni - Falasch
géo Ham

L'ILLUSTRATION
AUTOMOBILE
ET TOURISME
PRIX : 10 FRANCS
3 OCTOBRE 1936

## L'AFFAIR GEO HAM

In June of 1936, Delahaye commissioned Figoni & Falaschi to build an aerodynamic convertible on its Type 135 short chassis for the Paris Auto Salon in October, 1936. Mr. Pegnet, the director of Delahaye, approved the styling drawings in mid-June, and the chassis was delivered to the Figoni workshop in the last week of that month. Work began immediately. Figoni based the Type 135's styling on the streamlined designs he was already crafting in his shop, as well as the designs being produced by coachbuilders in Italy and Switzerland. He also took inspiration from the work of Russian designer Alexis Sakhoffski, whose automotive styling drawings were published in the January 1934 issue of *Esquire*.

On August 7, 1936, the well-known French painter Geo Ham contacted Figoni & Falaschi and began a dialog to build a streamlined coupé on a chassis of his selection. The coupé, like the Type 135 convertible, was to be displayed at the Paris Auto Salon of that year. Ham had also arranged for *L'Illustration* magazine to feature his car on the cover of its October issue, which would coincide with the Paris Auto Salon. A draft contract between Figoni & Falaschi and Ham was established on August 11, 1936. A few weeks later, at the end of the month, Ham came to the Figoni workshop with a single concept drawing of the body he wanted placed on a Delage chassis. The lines of this drawing were identical to those of the drawing eventually published in *L'Illustration*. The drawing's depiction of the front fenders was also very similar to that of several Figoni-produced drawings, which Figoni showed to Ham at their first meeting. The Figoni drawings were from the aerodynamic Delahaye convertible then under construction for the upcoming Paris Auto Salon.

Figoni never solicited Ham to help with the coachwork for the Delahaye convertible, and when Ham offered to collaborate on the project, his help was accepted but effected no substantial changes to the design. Ham's "involvement" came a month after work had begun, so the coachwork was already well underway according

*Facing page: Geo Ham concept drawing on the cover of the October 1936 issue of* L'Illustration, *a popular French magazine.*

*1937 Delahaye 135 M Roadster - Chassis No. 48666*

*1937 Delahaye 135 M Cabriolet - Chassis No. 48667*

*1938 Talbot-Lago T-150-C - Chassis No. 90019*

to the Delahaye-approved drawings. Ham's Delage chassis was not delivered until September 21, 1936, so it was not possible for Figoni to complete its new body for the October show.

At the opening of the 1936 Paris Auto Salon, when the Figoni-bodied Delahaye Type 135 convertible was displayed on a raised turntable at the Delahaye stand, it caused an instant sensation. The styling was fantastic: it accentuated the modernism and aerodynamic style that were to become Figoni's trademarks. However, on the morning of the car's debut, a heated dispute arose between Ham and Figoni over who had designed the coachwork. Later that day, Ham went to his lawyer and the Paris police and filed a complaint against Figoni for infringement of design. Figoni was served while on the Delahaye stand, and the Type 135 became subject to seizure. Ham then went to the Delahaye factory office and threatened to seize the car, claiming to be the designer. To add insult to injury, he even spoke with the French press and claimed not only that the car was of his design, but that Figoni's coachwork failed to follow his drawings.

That same day Mr. Falaschi, bending to pressure and wishing to avoid scandal and possible blackmail, managed to appease Ham. The peace pact, which was devised by Mr. Falaschi and Mr. Pegnet, denied Ham any rights to the car's design. In return, Figoni & Falaschi would pay the artist a fee of 500 French francs for each car sold with "his" coachwork. The Type 135 was able to remain on the stand until the end of the event, at which time Ali Khan purchased the car.

However, the dispute did not end there—friction still existed between the parties. Ham's name was on all promotional advertising, and a plaque naming him as a designer was placed on each of the eleven cars produced in the series. There was a great deal of bad blood and the case eventually went to court. At the trial, Ham's claim that he had supervised the construction of the Delahaye using his drawings was shown to be false. Figoni & Falaschi proved that the Delahaye had been built from the original Delahaye plans, which had been approved in June, weeks before Ham's involvement. Nineteen craftsmen from Figoni's shop testified to this point, and to the fact that Ham had not been at the factory directing them.

Things went badly for Ham: the judge threw out his claim of design infringement, and so he had to withdraw his complaint. Ham eventually apologized to Figoni, but with World War II looming on the horizon, the Figoni & Falaschi victory was not widely reported, and the dispute and resolution fell into obscurity. In the years that followed, the Ham myth was perpetuated as writers and owners saw the promotional materials and plaques that bore Ham's name. No one dug into the facts, and so the truth remained overlooked. However, it is our hope that this account of the events that took place before and after the 1936 Paris Auto Salon will set the record straight.

*— The facts in this narrative were obtained from the Figoni & Falaschi archives.*

*Facing page: Three styling variations of the 1936 Paris Auto Salon model. The top two are slightly different Delahaye Type 135s on short chassis. The bottom car is a Talbot-Lago on a longer chassis with a larger compartment for the driver. On the center car, note the Geo Ham signature plaque to the rear of the driver's door.*

# 1938 DELAHAYE 135 M

*CHASSIS 49150*

*COACHBUILDER: FIGONI & FALASCHI*

The Delahaye Type 135 was first presented at the 1934 Paris Auto Salon and came in several models, among them the Standard, Competition, and Competition Court (on a short chassis) versions. A variation of the Type 135 was the more powerful and sophisticated Type 135 M, produced in Standard, Competition, and MS versions.

This car was ordered by well-known explorer and businessman Casimir Jourde, a devotee of streamlined styling and a personal friend of Joseph Figoni. When World War II broke out, Jourde offered his large country estate in Brittany as a safe haven for the Figoni family. "It was thus," says Claude Figoni, "that after the occupation of France by German troops my grandmother, my sister, and I went from our home in Boulogne to the Château de Branféré for several months, awaiting the return of our parents who had left for the Dordogne." After the war, Jourde donated his property to the region, and it exists today as a zoo.

Jourde's Type 135 M, Chassis 49150, was one of eleven cars built in the Paris Auto Salon series between 1936 and 1939. Today, it is one of three surviving cars built on the standard wheelbase. Painted the same red hue as the V-12 Delahaye show car built for the 1938 Paris Auto Salon, it was equipped with three Solex downdraft carburetors and a Cotal transmission system. In 1939, the car was shipped to Bombay, India, where Jourde had business interests and where his car created quite a stir.

*Facing page: Chassis No. 49150 photographed while in India.*

60WW20

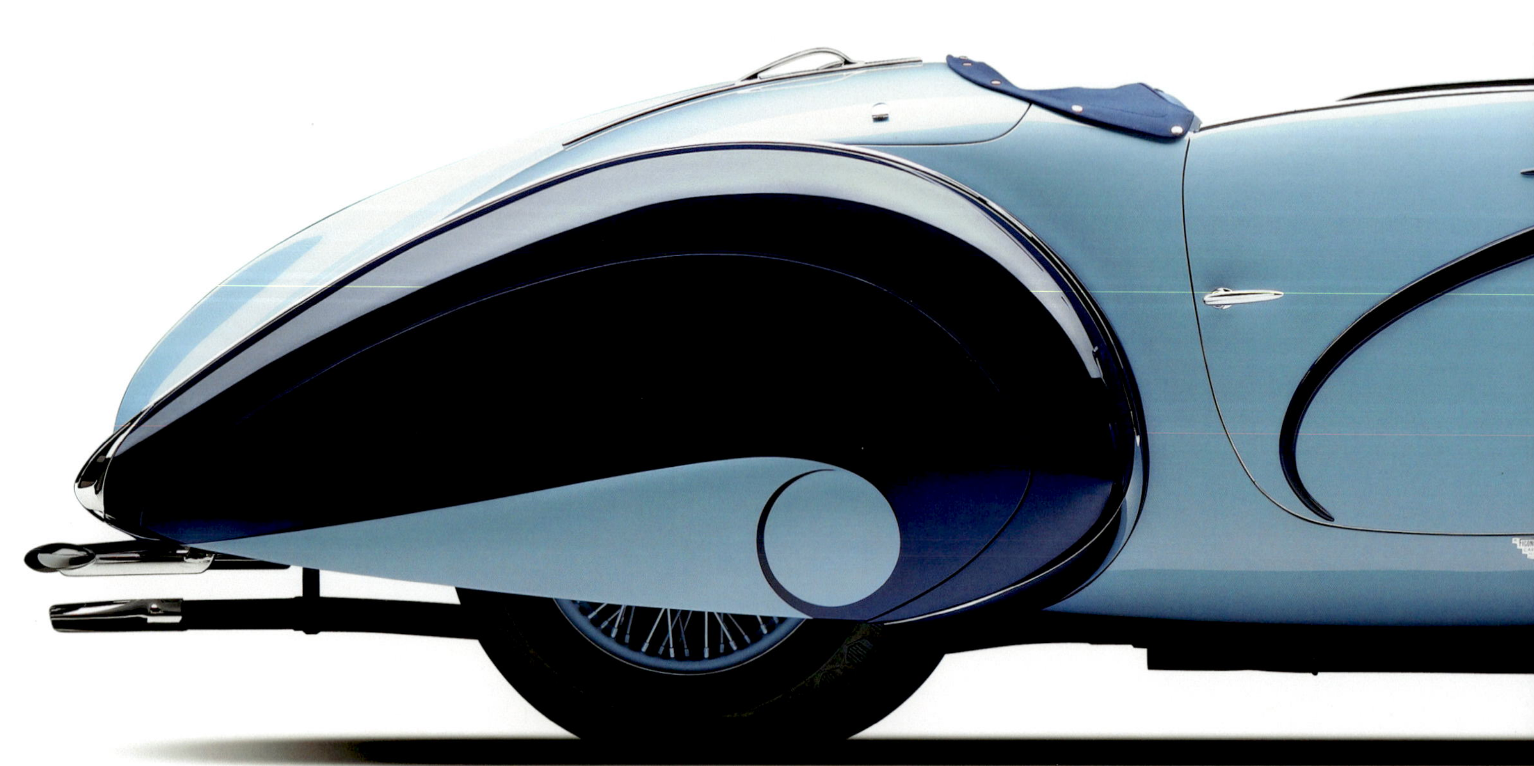

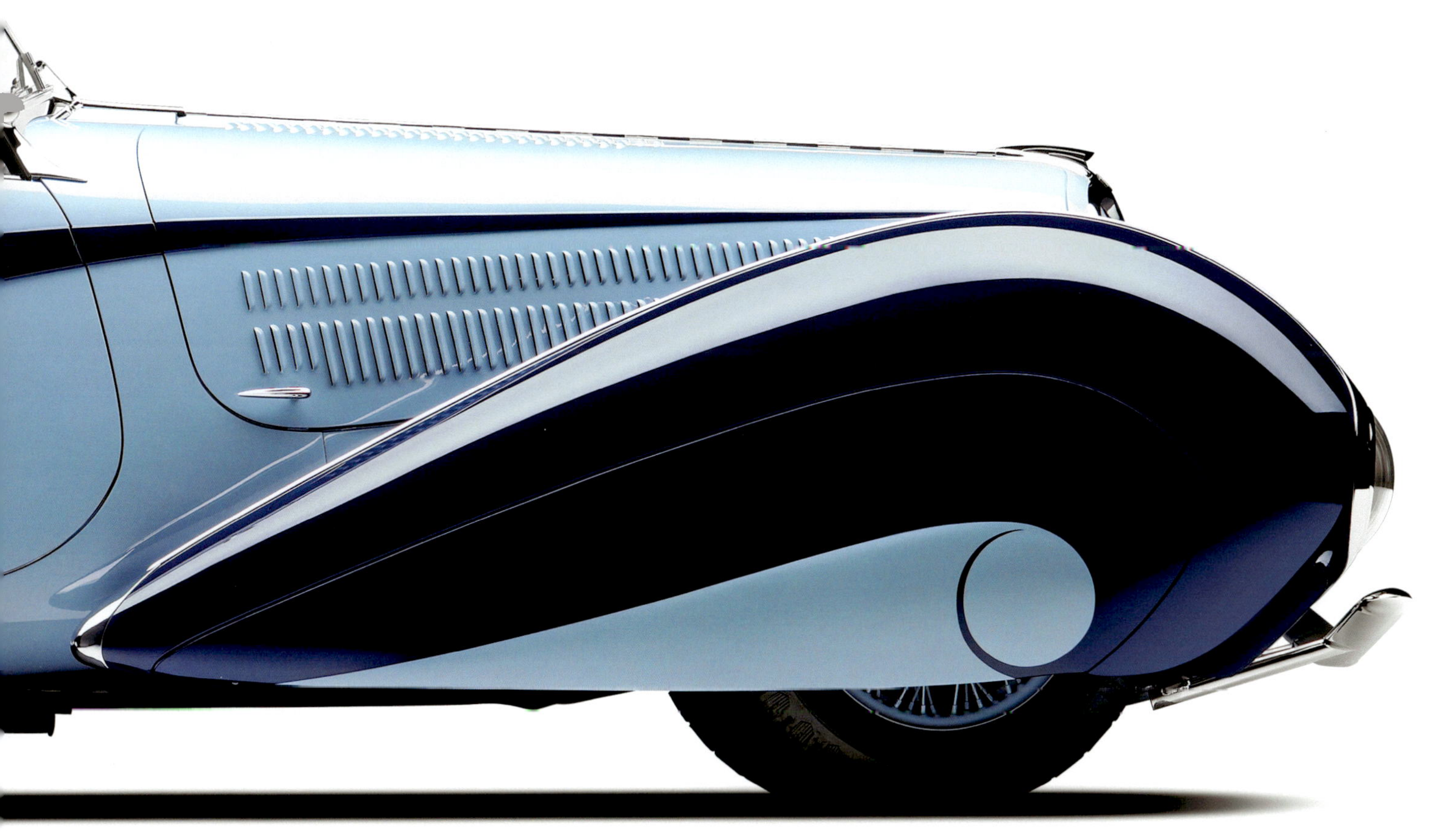

*Above: Hood handle with custom streamlined styling.*
*Facing page, top: The scalloped woodwork on the window sill is typical of Figoni's styling.*
*Facing page, bottom: The taillight is built into the chrome tip of the rear fender.*

*While in India, the car sustained some front end damage, and the built-in headlights were replaced with Marchal Aerolux lights in the valley between the front fenders. This was later corrected, with the assistance of Claude Figoni, when the car was restored in 2006.*

Jourde's Delahaye was soon purchased by Prince de Berae Mukarran Jah, who added it to his collection. He sold it many years later, although it is not known to whom, at which point the car fell from sight and into neglect. When it was finally rediscovered in 1982, it was sitting on wooden blocks in a garden shed in Jodhpur. An English dealer bought it in the mid-1980s, had it disassembled, and shipped it in crates to England, where it underwent a complete restoration. The original front end coachwork had been changed in India, where—according to Claude Figoni—the flush-mounted headlights were removed and replaced by externally mounted Marchal lights. The original design appears on page 26, while the modifications can be clearly appreciated in a photograph of the car taken in India and shown on the facing page. The English dealer, however, did not realize that alterations had been made, so the car was mistakenly restored as found. The interior was also redone with the help of vintage photographs supplied by the Figoni archive.

In 1989—after the restoration was complete—the car was taken to France and shown at the Bagatelle Concours d'Élégance, where it won First in Class, and Rétromobile, where it won Best of Show. It competed in the 1992 Pebble Beach Concours d'Élégance in the Delahaye exhibition, where Peter Mullin saw and fell in love with the cabriolet; he immediately added it to his collection. After being purchased by Mr. Mullin, Chassis 49150 went on to be named Most Elegant at the 1997 Le Cercle Concours d'Élégance held in Los Angeles and First in Class and Best of Show at the German Concours d'Élégance at Schloss Schwetzingen. An independent panel of judges at the German event also selected the Delahaye as "the best car in the world," a remarkable honor for a French car on foreign soil.

In 2006, the car underwent another restoration in California at the hands of Brian Hoyt. Under the guidance of Claude Figoni, it was returned to its original configuration, with recessed headlights and properly faired-in taillights. The cabriolet was shown again at the 2007 Pebble Beach and 2008 Amelia Island Concours d'Élégance, and it remains in the Mullin Collection.

# 1939 DELAHAYE 165

## *CHASSIS 60744*
## *COACHBUILDER: FIGONI & FALASCHI*

After the racing success of its Type 145, Delahaye created the production version, the 12-cylinder Type 165. Two Type 165s were built, and the first was shown in October 1938 at the Paris Auto Salon, the last salon before the war. It was a gorgeous Figoni & Falaschi speedster with fully enclosed front and rear pontoon fenders, a patented roll-down windshield, and a disappearing top. The car was afterwards sold to an English customer.

The second Delahaye Type 165 (Chassis 60744, coachbuilder number 750), which is now part of the Mullin Collection, was created a year later· for the 1939 New York World's Fair. It was a struggle to finish the car on schedule, and in order for it to arrive in time to be displayed at the French Pavilion, it ultimately had to be shipped before the engine was completed. The bright red streamlined cabriolet was an immediate success at the fair, drawing large crowds and much media attention.

The car showcased Figoni's characteristic repeated voluptuous curves in what has come to be known as the Teardrop style. The hood had a cutout so that the empty engine shell (which appeared to be a completed engine) could be viewed, and the firewall was engine-turned, as were the valve covers—all of which made for a showy display.

The fair was so successful that it was extended through 1940. By that time Hitler's armies were occupying France, so the ownership of the French cars in New York was unclear. As a result, U.S. Customs impounded those cars, including the Type 165, until the ownership issues could be resolved. Chassis 60744 sat in a warehouse in New York City until 1946, when it was put up for sale. It was purchased by Roger Barlow, who took it to Beverly Hills, California, and displayed it at International Motors, his new exotic car dealership. It was difficult to find parts for the Delahaye V-12's empty

*Workmen at the Figoni workshop completing the 1939 New York World's Fair car. The boy in the middle is Claude Figoni.*

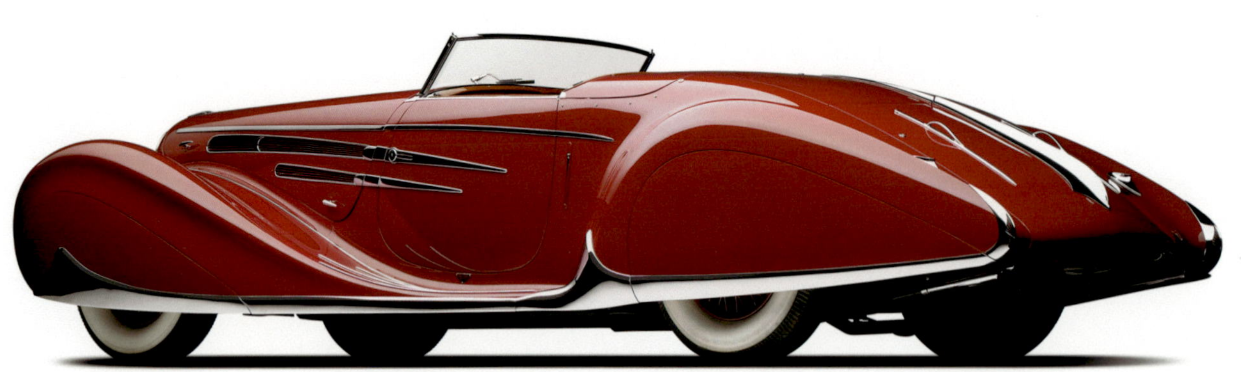

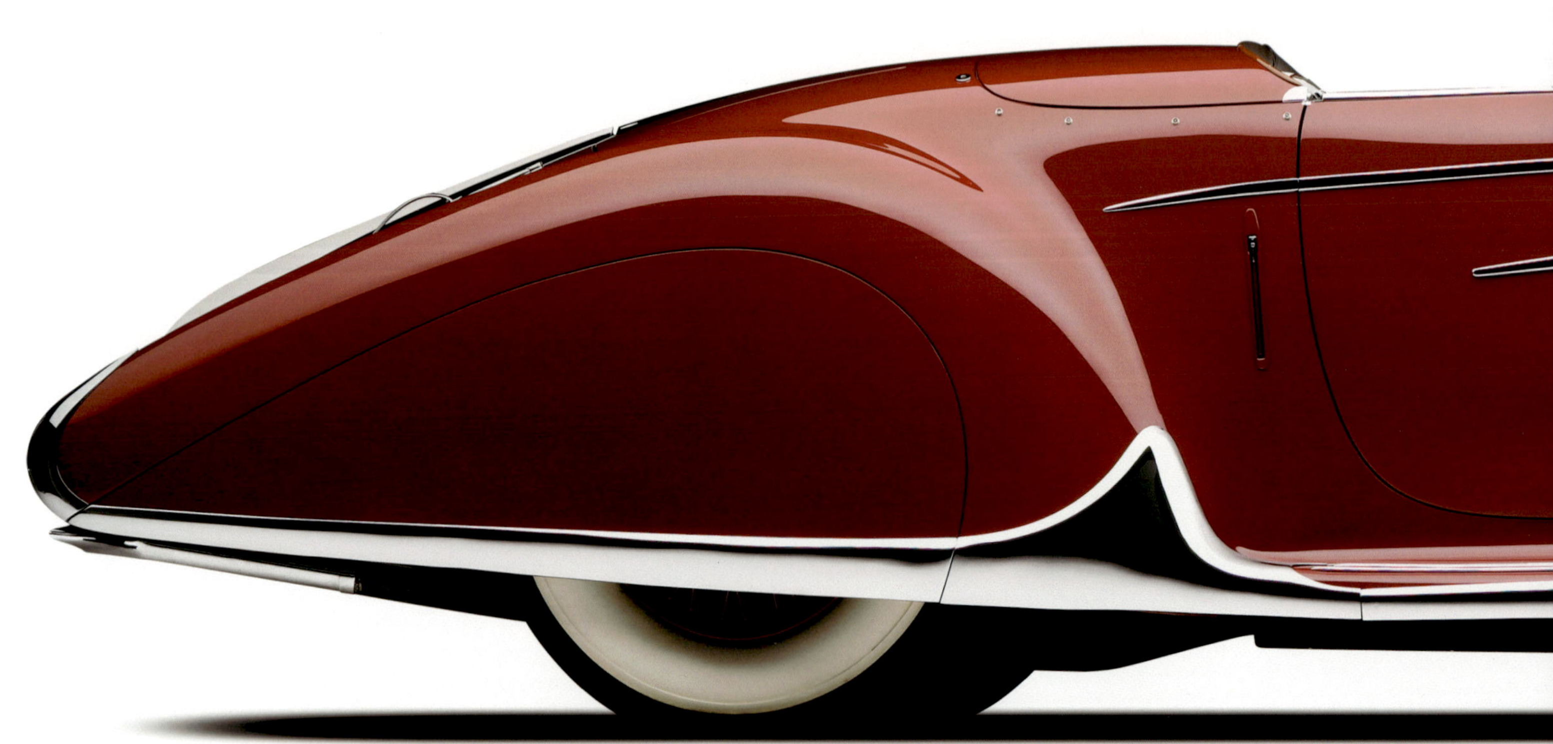

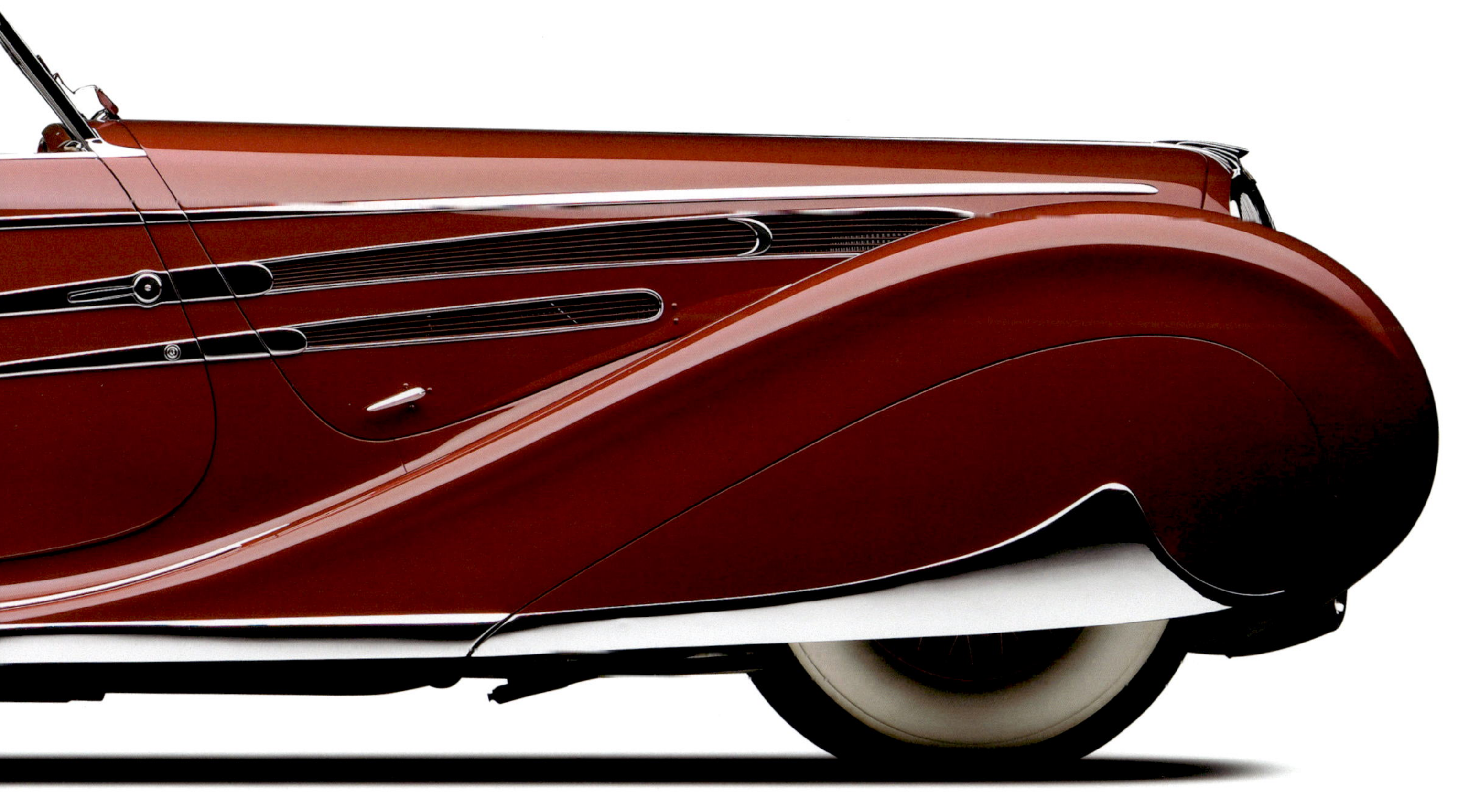

FIG. 1

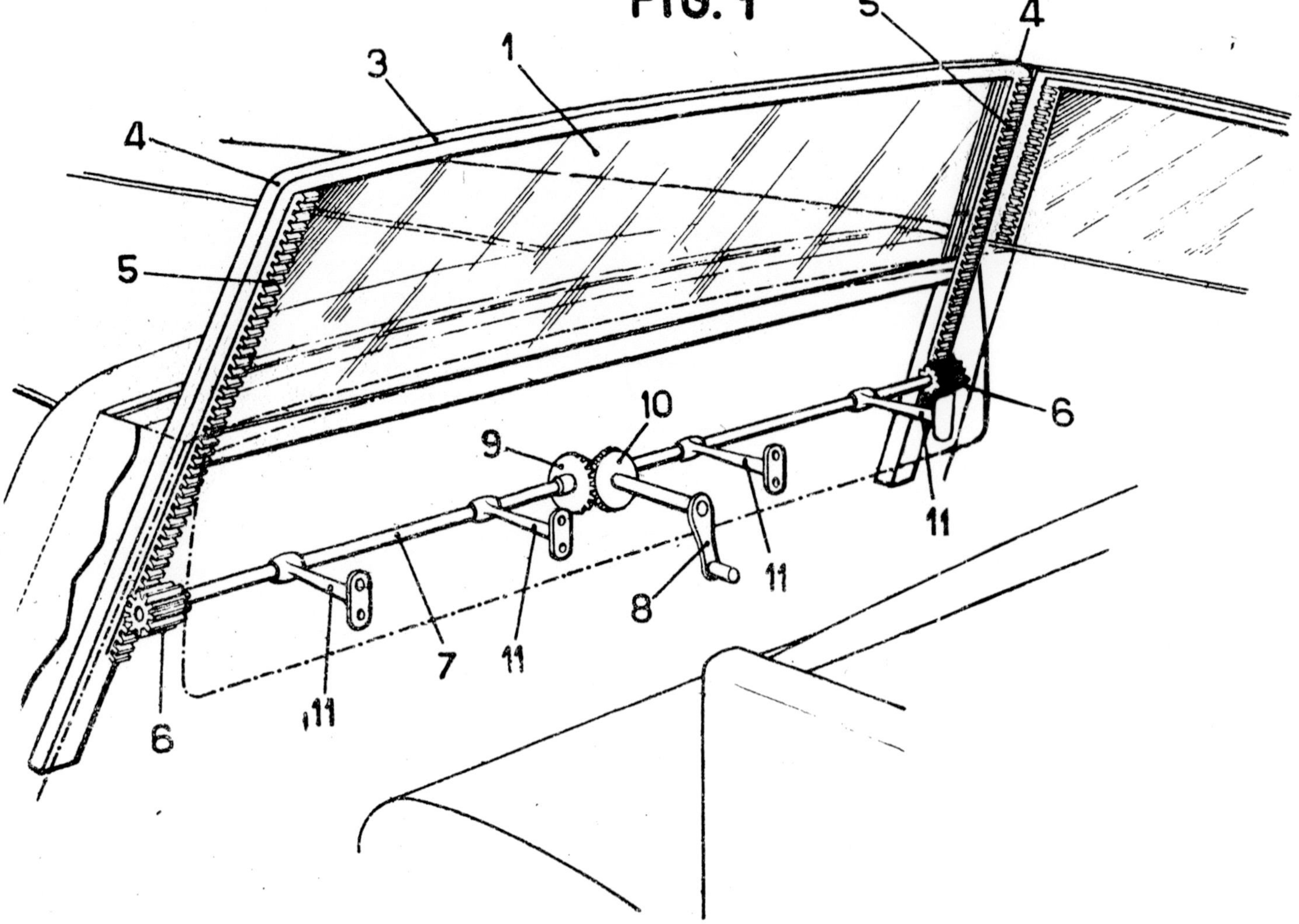

3 1 4 5 5 4 6 9 10 11 11 8 7 11 11 6

FIG. 3

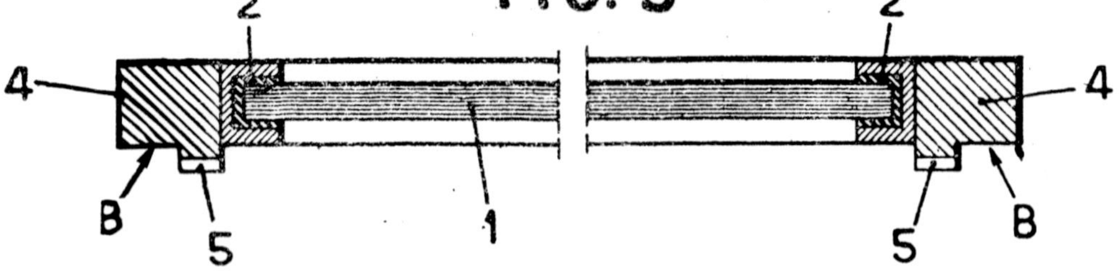

2 2 4 4 B 5 1 5 B

FIG. 2

12 12 5 4 6 10 7 9 11 8

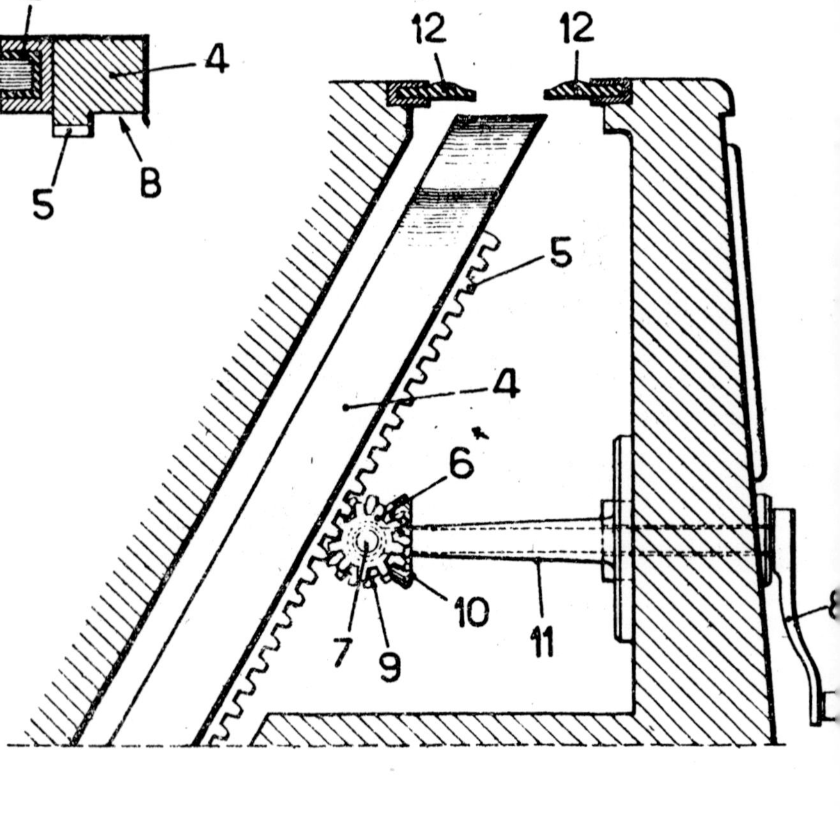

*Facing page: Joseph Figoni patented many innovations in automotive coachwork. This unique design for a roll-down front windshield was used in the 1939 New York World's Fair Delahaye Type 165. The patent (number 828.020) was requested on October 19, 1937, and granted May 9, 1938.*

engine shell, so when Vivian Corradini, a wealthy businessman from New York, wanted one installed, Barlow decided to work with what he could get and installed a special Cadillac engine with up to 210 hp. Corradini outbid several movie stars to purchase the car for $12,000 in 1946. When the car left for The Big Apple, the empty V-12 engine shell remained behind at International Motors, displayed on an engine stand in the showroom, where it was often seen by race car driver Phil Hill, who was an employee there prior to his racing career. The engine was eventually sold to New York collector Robert Grier, who sold it to Lew Gotthainer of New Jersey in 1951. In 1970, car dealer Uwe Hucke purchased the engine shell and immediately resold it to Count Hubertus von Doenhoff of Germany, who held onto it for the next decade or so.

After it was purchased by Corradini, Chassis 60744 disappeared for a few years until it resurfaced in Honolulu; it was found, repainted black, in the lot of a used car dealer who sold exotic models. In 1951 L.N. Nevels, a lieutenant in the naval reserve who had just been called up for the Korean War, saw this car and fell in love with it. He brought it home to his wife, who was pregnant with their third child, and they used it as a family car while stationed on Oahu. Said Mrs. Nevels, "This automobile was a marvel, with its wind-down windshield and the richest, thickest chrome plating I have ever seen on any car other than a Rolls-Royce...Every policeman between the Scholdfield Barracks and Pearl Harbor knew that car!" Lt. Nevels and his wife drove the Type 165 for three years before selling it to an enlisted man, who took it to the West Coast in 1953.

After its return to the mainland, the story of the Type 165 again becomes a little vague, but it is reported that the enlisted man transported the car to California, and after some time took it to a shop in Fresno. However, he soon passed away and his wife did not pay the bill, so Chassis 60744 became property of the garage and remained so for a number of years, during which time the Cadillac engine was removed and lost, along with several other parts of the car. Around 1981, Jim Hull, a California-based French car collector and associate of Peter Mullin, was attending the Monterey Historic Automobile Races. There, he met a couple who told him they knew of a man in Fresno who owned an

*After purchasing the car from International Motors in Los Angeles, Mr. Corradini says goodbye to the West Coast and heads to New York City.*

*The Type 165 in front of International Motors after being purchased from U.S. Customs by Roger Barlow. Note: American bumpers were added to make the car street legal.*

amazing Delahaye. They'd seen the car by the airport, parked next to a yellow tow truck. Hull followed the lead, driving to Fresno and crisscrossing every street near the airport until he found the car sticking out of a small garage, and sure enough, the yellow tow truck was parked nearby. Al Brewer, the tow truck driver, was also the Delahaye's owner. He'd purchased the car for $1,200 in the 1970s from the garage where the enlisted man had left it. Hull set out to buy the Delahaye, but not before Brewer's wife researched the model and realized exactly how valuable it was. After five years of negotiations, Hull and Mr. Mullin were finally able to strike a deal with the Brewers.

That same year, 1986, Hull and Mr. Mullin were able to acquire the original V-12 engine shell from Count Doenhoff. The two men hoped to restore the car in time for its fiftieth anniversary, and to debut it at the 1989 Pebble Beach Concours d'Élégance, but the work took longer than hoped because it took time to machine all-new V-12 engine parts. The engine was completed by Crosthwaite and Gardiner in England using the original factory drawings and the coachwork was restored in California. Restoration was finally completed in the summer of 1992, just in time for the Pebble Beach Concours d'Élégance of that year. The car has since been shown around the world, and it consistently wins major prizes.

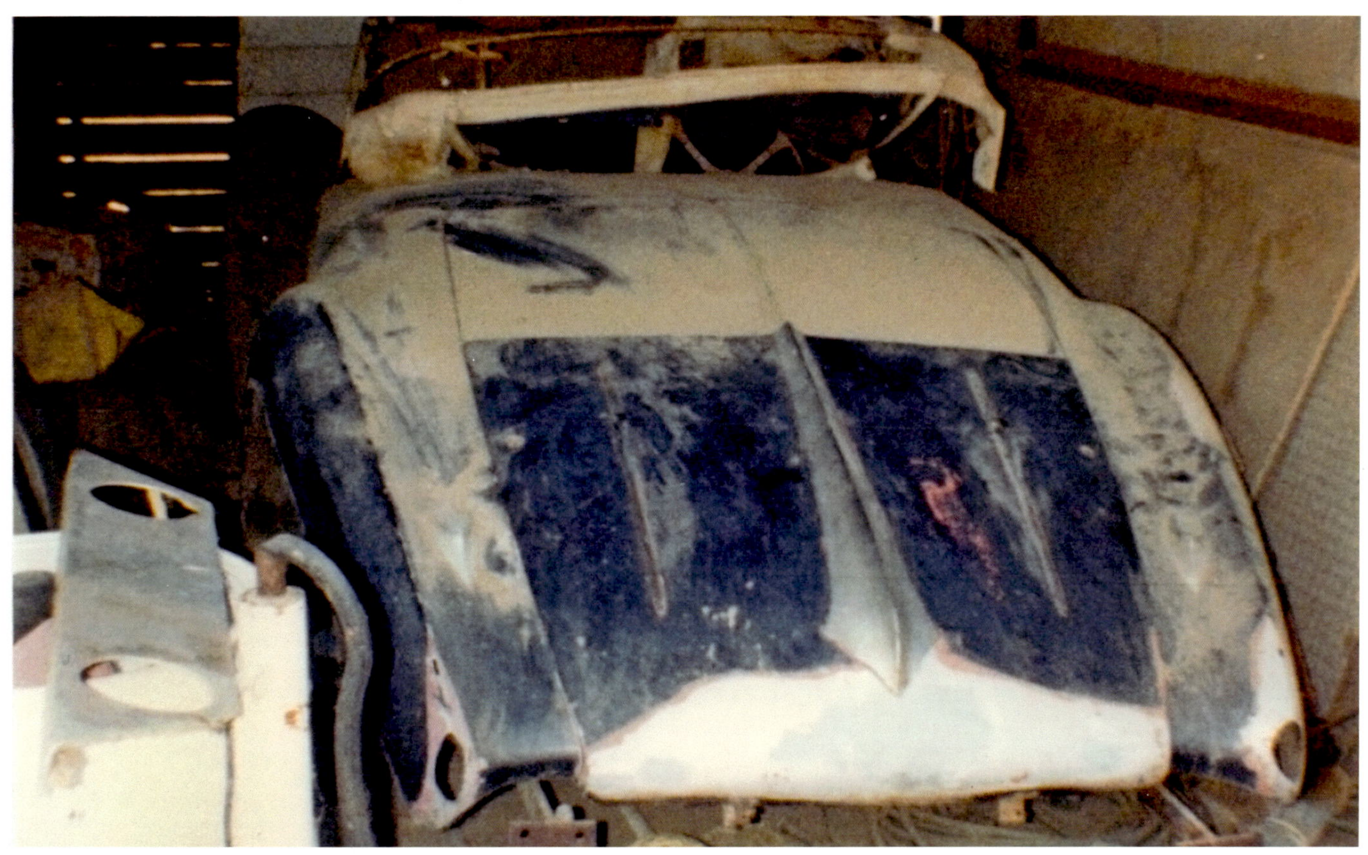

*Top: This is the state in which Jim Hull found the Type 165 in Fresno.*
*Bottom: The car after being pulled out of the garage. In the natural light, the black (not blue) paint job is evident. Note: Some of the original red paint can be seen on the lower left fender.*

# 1948 DELAHAYE 135 MS

## *CHASSIS 800494*

## *COACHBUILDER: HENRI CHAPRON*

The Mullin Collection includes four examples of the Delahaye Type 135 MS, including the subject of this story, Chassis 800494, which was produced in 1948 and designed by Henri Chapron as a four-passenger coupé. Recent research in the Chapron archives has confirmed that this particular car was among those displayed at the 1948 Paris Auto Salon, adding to its historical value as an unrestored Delahaye.

In 1985, after a number of years out of the spotlight, this Type 135 MS re-emerged as the property of Robert Drollinger, who said he had purchased it in the late 1970s from David Sterling, a dealer in Black Rock, California. Drollinger kept the car in the garage of an old apartment building near the La Brea tar pits in Los Angeles. Convinced that the country was headed for an economic crisis, he wanted to turn all of his assets into gold coins, so he sold the Delahaye to Jim Hull and Peter Mullin for a modest price, since the car was not in running condition and had been sitting on blocks for many years. Twenty-three years later, when Hull spoke to the gentleman again at a social gathering for classic car lovers, the Delahaye's former owner confessed that he still had all the gold he had managed to amass. He was killed a short time later in a car accident, still in possession of his bullion bulwark against an economic downturn.

When Mr. Mullin bought the car, he initially intended to use it to provide spare parts for other Delahayes in his collection. The car was in almost entirely original condition; nearly nothing was missing. All the knobs and gauges were still in place, the engine compartment was absolutely untouched, the wiring was factory produced, it had a sunroof—an unusual feature—and it even had all of the chrome trim with its original Chapron script. The Chapron body tag was missing, but the shop build number was found stamped on all the chrome pieces of the car. The paint was still the original blue and had not been washed in many years. When they received the car, Mr. Mullin and his restorer considered getting it into running condition but came to the conclusion that doing so would compromise the patina of the engine compartment. The interior was found to be just as original; the seats, the headliners, the carpet binding, the door panels, the carpeting, and the rubber trim, although worn and decayed, provide invaluable guidance for anyone who wishes to undertake the renovation of a Delahaye.

As the years have passed, the authenticity of the coupé has become far more important than its value as a possible provider of spare parts. This untouched example now serves as a priceless reference, used by experts and enthusiasts alike who want to know how a truly original Type 135 MS appears.

*Chassis 800494 as it appears in its "barn find" setting at the Mullin Automotive Museum.*

DELAHAYE
GFA

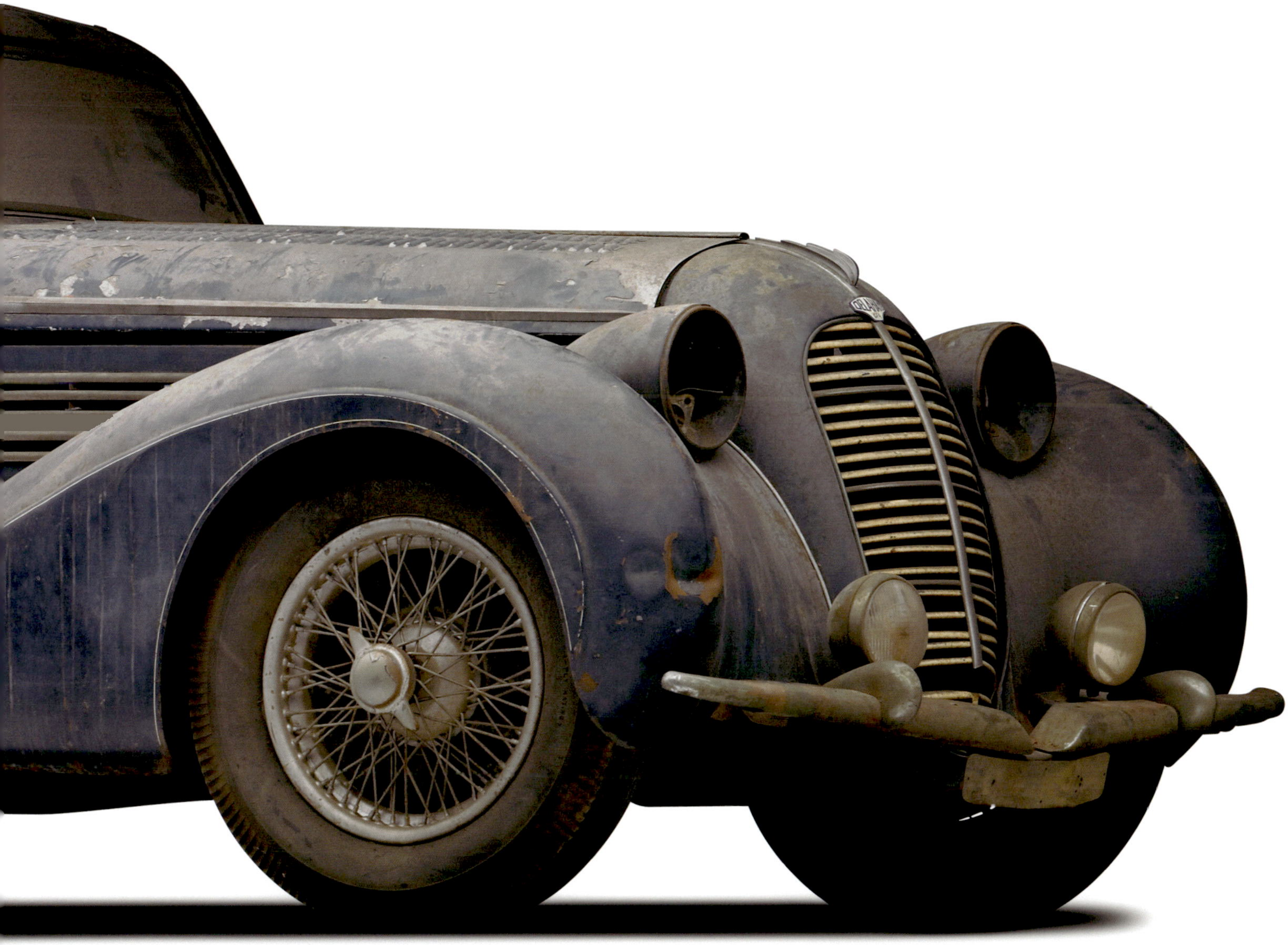

*Because this Delahaye Type 135 MS was the Paris Auto Salon Car of 1948, the Henri Chapron script was larger than usual to make the coachbuilder easily recognizable to prospective clients.*

*The remarkable aspect of this car is its originality. Its state is deteriorated, but original and complete.*

# 1949 DELAHAYE 135 MS

## *CHASSIS 800727*

## *COACHBUILDER: HENRI CHAPRON*

The Mullin Collection also has another highly original Delahaye Type 135 MS: Chassis 800727, body number 6643. This car was ordered in April 1948 and produced in March 1949 for Henri Gugolz, a dealer of Delahayes and Delages in Zurich, Switzerland, who intended to show it at all the major concours in his country. The details of the next twenty-five years are unknown, but in 1976, it was purchased by Swiss collector Walter Grell, who placed it in his museum in Rheinfelden, where it was carefully preserved for a quarter of a century. In 2000 the car was put up for auction in Monaco by Barrett-Jackson and Coys of Kensington and was bought for the Mullin Collection.

Chassis 800727 is a Chapron cabriolet with elegant post-war styling rooted in classic French lines. Henri Chapron called this his Vedette style: a cabriolet with covered rear wheels, chrome trim, and a top that disappears into the coachwork when folded down. The exterior paint remains the blue-gray combination chosen by Chapron, who called the hue "Nice" blue in reference to the premier city of the Côte d'Azur. The car also has its original interior; the gauges are a little faded and the knobs are worn, but everything works and has a comfortable feel. The seats are upholstered in blue and white leather with white piping, and the varnished wood frame surrounding the seat backs matches the trim on the doorsills and dashboard surround, each element combining to create a luxurious interior. The whole car is a perfect example of the custom work at which Chapron excelled, and it has the kind of patina that collectors covet.

*This was one of Chapron's promotional drawings to show potential customers the possibilities for their new Vedette cabriolet. Following pages: Original Chapron build sheets for body number 6643. Note the paint, leather, and cloth color samples.*

DELAHAYE
GFA

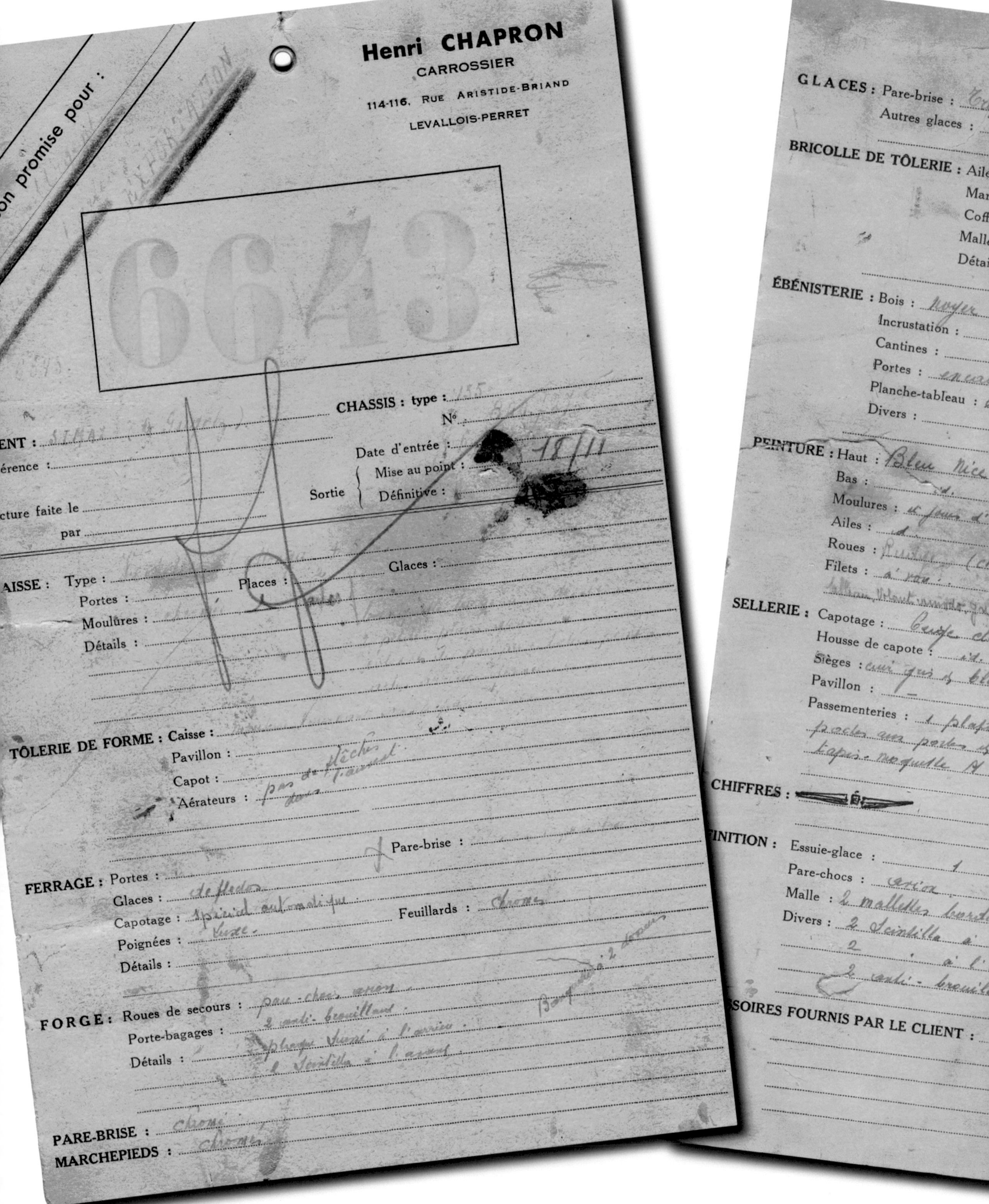

on promise pour :
Henri CHAPRON
CARROSSIER
114-116, Rue Aristide-Briand
LEVALLOIS-PERRET
6643
CHASSIS : type :
N°
Date d'entrée :
Sortie
Mise au point :
Définitive :
ENT :
érence :
cture faite le
par
AISSE : Type :
Portes :
Moulures :
Détails :
Places :
Glaces :
TÔLERIE DE FORME : Caisse :
Pavillon :
Capot :
Aérateurs :
Pare-brise :
FERRAGE : Portes :
Glaces :
Capotage :
Poignées :
Détails :
Feuillards :
FORGE : Roues de secours :
Porte-bagages :
Détails :
PARE-BRISE :
MARCHEPIEDS :
GLACES : Pare-brise :
Autres glaces :
BRICOLLE DE TÔLERIE : Ailes
Marc
Coffr
Malle
Détails
ÉBÉNISTERIE : Bois : noyer
Incrustation :
Cantines :
Portes :
Planche-tableau :
Divers :
PEINTURE : Haut : Bleu Nice
Bas :
Moulures :
Ailes :
Roues :
Filets :
SELLERIE : Capotage :
Housse de capote :
Sièges :
Pavillon :
Passementeries :
CHIFFRES :
FINITION : Essuie-glace :
Pare-chocs :
Malle : 2 mallettes
Divers : 2 Scintilla
SSOIRES FOURNIS PAR LE CLIENT :

6643. Modification de la planche de bord

Quincaillerie

| | | | |
|---|---|---|---|
| | | 100 | |
| 060 | laiton cuivre | | |
| 3 | soudure étain | 31 | |
| | – autogène | 81 | |
| 700 | triton | 180 | |
| | | 238 | |
| | Minuterie Marchal | | |
| | interrupteurs | 490 | |
| | cheminées | 982 | |
| | supports lamps } | | |
| | lamps | 375 | |
| | inverseur flèche | 320 | |
| | fil 16/10 | 90 | |
| | gaine de 21 | 180 | |
| | " de 7 | 182 | |
| | cosse de 5 | 176 | |
| | colliers bowden | 40 | |
| | résistance de robinet de batterie | 20 | |
| | | 134 | |
| | garniture boutons plexiglas | 2840 | |
| | bis et chrome pl de bord | | |
| | guillochage -do- | 480 | |
| | garniture appareils Seignol | 1000 | |
| | | 16128 | 20160 |
| | | 23617 | |

tolerie
Montage
ébénisterie
mécanique
électricité

prix de revient brut 48.880.
vente. 65.000.

ouies sur le capot
de malle
inclinée
à l'arrière
avant Luxe
vide-poche - cendrier
cde 17/9
métallisé (voir de Rola)
non
Delahaye
voir Madet
tous tissus plaque de Poterie
la moulure
banquette à 2 dossiers
Accoudoir central :
1
plume
(luxe)

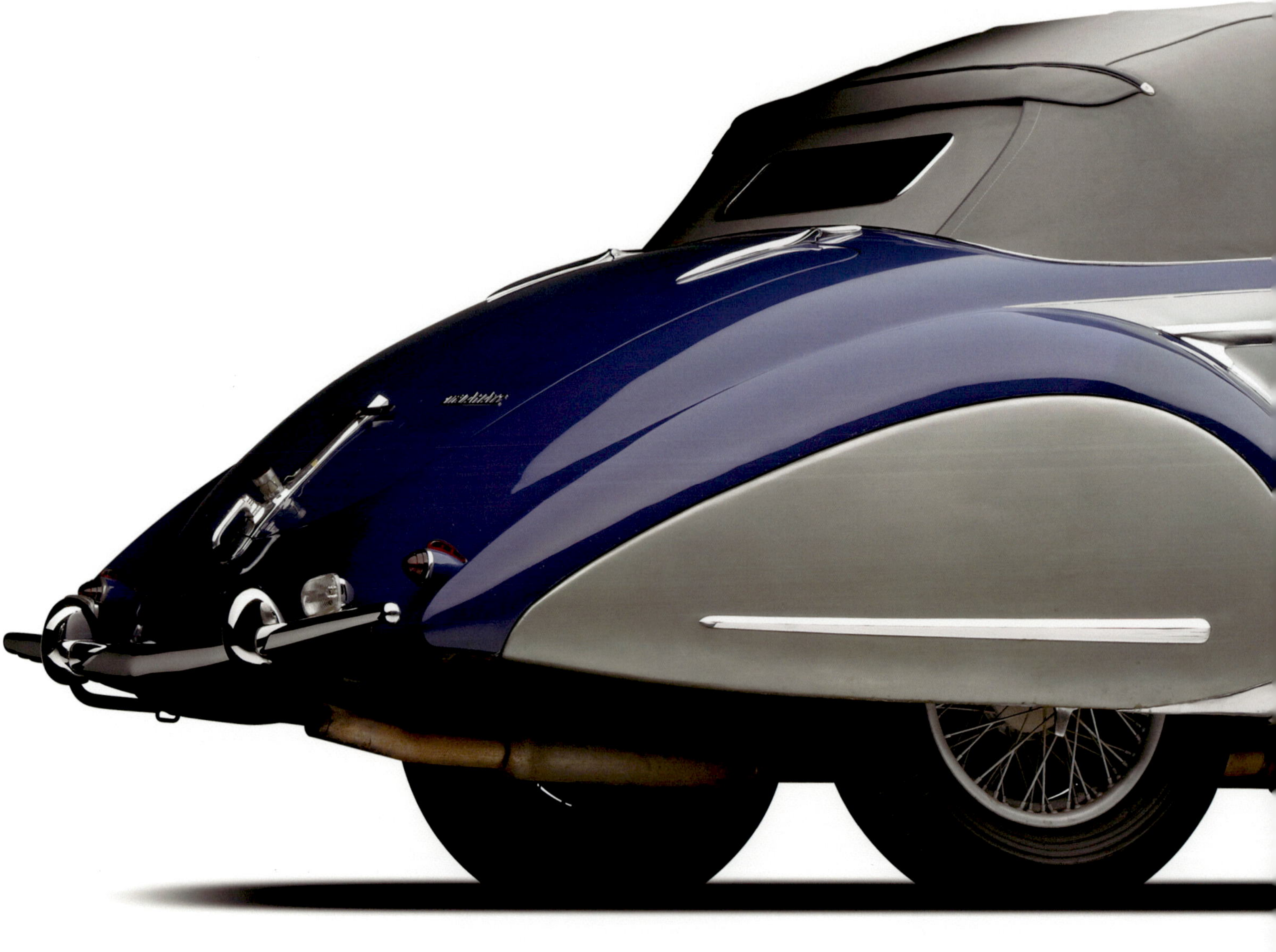

# 1951 DELAHAYE 235

*CHASSIS 818005*

*COACHBUILDER: JACQUES SAOUTCHIK*

Jacques Saoutchik, a Russian émigré who became one of France's premier coachbuilders, displayed Chassis 818005 on his stand at the October 1951 Paris Auto Salon, where it was presented for the 1952 model year. It was placed on a rotating turntable and from this place of honor impressed the media and public alike. In spite of excellent reviews, however, buyers were intimidated by its high price, which was double that of the competing Jaguar XK-120.

The car was the fifth of the eighty-four Type 235 chassis built by Delahaye between 1951 and 1954. Chassis 818005 had the first of four Type 235 custom coachwork bodies by Saoutchik. It was constructed from a unique combination of aluminum, which was applied to the body from the doors forward, and steel, which was applied to the rear. This method provided balance and at the same time reduced the car's weight.

The Type 235 was intended as a new model for Delahaye, designed and styled for the post-war market. In fact, it was a slightly modernized pre-war Type 135 MS chassis: although a new grill was added, the old 3.5-liter motor was preserved with slight modifications to the camshaft and carburetors, which boosted the horsepower to 150. The car's top speed was 169 kph.

By that time, almost all car manufacturers in continental Europe (and the rest of the world) had adopted a standard of left-hand drive, but Delahaye chose not to. The right-hand drive feature of the Type 235 diminished its chances in the United States, one of the largest markets for expensive luxury cars. A second limiting factor was, again, its exorbitant price. As a result, the model did not revive the fortunes of the Delahaye company as hoped, and only a handful of cars were sold over the next three years. The company closed soon thereafter in 1954.

Chassis 818005 was owned by a French collector for nearly fifty years and was only stored away when it stopped working in 1964. It was rediscovered in France in 2006 by Jacques Harguindeguy, a collector from Walnut Creek, California, who was always on the lookout for another streamlined French car. He soon got it running again and displayed it in its original condition at the Pebble Beach Concours d'Élégance of August 2007. When Harguindeguy (affectionately known as "Frenchy") died a month later, his car was bought by Peter Mullin, who had it completely restored and shown at the Pebble Beach Concours d'Élégance of 2009.

DELAHAYE
235

*Above: The Delahaye Type 235 at the Paris Auto Salon on the Delahaye stand in October 1951. This car, as well as those on the opposite page, share the same grill design, making them immediately recognizable as Delahayes.*

*Facing page, top: Antem, a small Parisian coachbuilder, made this body for a Delahaye Type 235 in 1951.*

*Facing page, bottom: Chapron-bodied Type 235 Delahaye from 1951. Note: The convertible top is folded down, resting flat and creating a clean and modern look.*

*The motor of the Delahaye Type 235 is similar to that of the Type 135 MS but develops a little more horsepower.*

*The gauges of the post-war Delahaye were updated to give the car a more modern look.*

4
3
2
1

# DELAHAYE RACE CARS

*Facing page: Delahaye Type 145 race cars numbers 1 and 2 at Le Mans on June 18 and 19, 1938; both cars raced for The Écurie Bleue team. Car 1, driven, by René Dreyfus and Louis Chiron, was gridded in first place but abandoned the race in lap 23. Car 2, driven by Gianfranco Comotti and Albert Divo, abandoned the race in lap 7.*

The Delahaye models that made the company famous on the racetrack between 1934 and 1952 were its Types 135, 138, 145, and 175. All were driven by many of the most famous drivers of the day and performed exceptionally well. It is extraordinary to consider that while Bugatti was producing hundreds of racing cars, Delahaye made its name with only a handful. Before the outbreak of World War II, the company had broken more than eighteen world and international class records and won numerous grand prix.

On October 13, 1935, at the Paris Auto Salon for the 1936 model year, Delahaye introduced several of the models that would make it famous, although the cars' naming conventions have caused quite a bit of confusion over the years. The first models were the Types 135 Coupe des Alps and the 138 Sport, although the latter was renamed midyear to the 135 Sport. Both had a straight 6-cylinder, 3.227-liter engine with three carburetors that could develop 113 hp at 3600 rpm. A manual 4-speed transmission was standard, as well as a Wilson pre-selector gearbox, all of which came to around 3,500 French francs; once the custom roadster body was added, the price rose to between 47,350 and 49,300 French francs. Delahaye enlarged the engine in 1936, increasing its displacement to 3.557 liters and enabling it to develop 120 hp at 4,200 rpm. This size became the standard for the remainder of the Type 135 model run, both before and after the war. The chassis of the Sport and Coupe des Alpes were the same length, measuring 2.95 meters. Although these models were not part of the Delahaye Factory Team, nor built as race cars per se, both were used in rallies with some success by amateurs and professionals alike.

A short chassis version of the Type 135, the Chassis Court, became available in 1936; it measured 2.70 meters in length and usually had a 4-speed manual transmission. Approximately fifty of these short chassis were built in the pre-war period, and none were built after the war. Several wonderful bodies were created on this chassis by Figoni & Falaschi, such as the Paris Auto Salon cars of 1935 through 1939. Henri

*Delahaye Type 135 S with factory racing engine at the 1936 Grand Prix de l'ACF; note the three Solex side-draft carburetors and large oil fill on top of the valve covers.*

Chapron also designed a handful of lovely Type 135 Chassis Court coupés and roadsters, some of which still exist today.

Particularly dependable was the Type 135 S (*surbaissé*), fourteen of which were manufactured in 1936. The example in the Peter Mullin collection, Chassis 47190, was ordered by Eugène Chaboud in March of 1937. The car's first outings took place later that year at the Tunisia Grand Prix and the Bône Grand Prix (in Algeria), although it did not finish high enough to make the records. Chaboud and race car driver Jean Trémoulet drove the Type 135 S in numerous races over the next two years, including the 1937 Grand Prix de l'ACF, where it placed sixth; the 1937 Marne Grand Prix, where it placed sixth again; the 1938 Antwerp Grand Prix, where it placed second; and most impressively, the 1938 Le Mans Grand Prix, where it placed first. For the 1938 season, Chassis 47190 was outfitted with a new, ugly, but demonstrably aerodynamic front nose section. Unfortunately, just three weeks after winning at Le Mans, Trémoulet crashed the car while competing in the 24 Heures de Spa-Francorchamps. Although the driver received only minor injuries, the Type 135 S was significantly damaged.

Before the end of 1938, John Snow of Australia purchased the Delahaye from Chaboud. Snow had it restored in Europe, then raced it at Brooklands and Le Mans, although it did not finish either race. It was shipped to Australia in 1939 and finished fourth at the Grand Prix of Australia with the best lap time. At the Bathurst Road Race, it had the fastest road time and came in second overall under the Australian handicap system.

DE·201

*Arthur Wylee, on right, driving Delahaye Chassis 47190 on Penrith Speedway in Australia in 1939.*

SC 202

*A post-war photo of John Crouch seated in his Delahaye after purchasing it from Mr. Snow. The location is believed to be in Bathurst, Australia.*

The car then went through several peaceful years. It was sold to John Crouch in 1940. While in his possession, it took eighth place at the 1948 Australian Grand Prix at Point and first place at the 1949 Australian Grand Prix. The Delahaye was later sold to Dick Bland, who entered it in the 1951 Australian Grand Prix for a second place finish.

Then disaster struck again: the truck bringing the Delahaye back to the garage caught fire, and the car was severely damaged. It was sold and changed hands several times before being purchased by Ian Polson, a British car collector and restorer, in 1968. He shipped it back to England and spent years carefully refurbishing his find.

After such a hazardous existence, it is remarkable that Chassis 47190 survived at all. Perhaps its endurance can be attributed to the admiration it inspired in its owners, as well as to their fondness for tinkering with old race cars. Polson sold the Delahaye in 1994 to John Ruston, and it was from Mr. Ruston that Peter Mullin finally purchased the car in 1999. Chassis 47190 now races at vintage car events.

JANVIER
RALLYE DE
MONTE CARLO
MARS
RALLYE FEMININ
PARIS S RAPHAEL
AVRIL
RALLYE PARIS
NICE
COURSE
MAI
HEURES
MARSEILLE
1936
LA 135 SPORT DEL
et 7 Rec

In addition to the dependable 6-cylinder Type 135 S, Delahaye also developed the Type 145, a powerful 12-cylinder model that would enjoy a particularly brilliant racing career. A second factor of the company's good fortune on the track was its association with the Écurie Bleue, a racing stable owned by American heiress Lucy Schell and her husband, Laury. Both were dedicated racers and often pressured Monsieur Charles to provide the Écurie Bleue with the latest and fastest Delahaye models ahead of all other customers, even those who had been faithful to the marque for many years. One of the motivations behind the development of Type 145 for the Schell team was the Million Franc Prize.

The story of the Million Franc Prize begins with the charged atmosphere of pre-World War II Europe. In the years that led up to the war, when Nazi Germany and its Fascist ally Italy were ramping up their military forces, sporting events were seen as metaphorical struggles between democracy and the totalitarian powers. So when the ACF changed its formula for the 1937 season, dictating that engines could henceforth be as large as 4.5 liters, unsupercharged, French marques such as Delahaye and Talbot-Lago saw their chance: although they lacked the time and resources to produce supercharged models, they would still be able to compete with German cars on a more even footing. The fundamental question was whether the French could build a 4.5-liter unsupercharged car that could beat the supercharged German competition.

Recognizing that a French success would be a political coup, the French government and the ACF organized a challenge: one million French francs—raised through a tax on each individual driver's license—would be awarded to the first car to break the 1934 record set by Louis Chiron, who had driven an Alfa Romeo at the Montlhéry racetrack at an average speed of 146.508 km/hr over 200 km. The record had to be broken by midnight of August 31, 1937.

Lucy Schell decided to fund Delahaye's effort in the race and ordered four Type 145s for the Écurie Bleue with very different and strictly utilitarian designs. These were Chassis 48771, 48772, 48773, and 48772-3, all with metal alloy coachwork that tightly sheathed the chassis, plus snub-nosed grilles with no frills or flourishes.

The engineers at the factory never tested the cars in a wind tunnel—they relied instead on their experience and intuition, the power of the Type 145s' unsupercharged 4.5-liter, V-12 engines, and the aerodynamic properties of the low-slung and well-balanced chassis. To promote sales of its touring models, Delahaye also intended to produce a detuned or sports car version of the Type 145, relying on the free publicity generated by the race.

By the beginning of July, Jean François and René Dreyfus were at the Montlhéry racetrack almost daily. The necessary speed had to top the old record for sixteen laps, or 200 km, from a standing start. To achieve the average, the driver had to make very careful calculations.

In an unpublished 1973 interview with Jean-Paul Caron, Dreyfus explained that the Schell-commissioned chassis selected for the race (Chassis 48771) was lightened as much as possible.

> *We kept tinkering, changing things here and there; we worked on the brakes, we worked on everything to try to increase the power. At one point I had a rather stern discussion with Jean François and told him that I couldn't go through the Ascari bend at more than a given speed. He didn't agree with me, and so I told him, "It's very simple, take the car, get in, take my goggles, and you'll see." So he got into the car, took my goggles, left, and after two or three laps, he stopped, saying he was very sorry but that he couldn't reach that speed, that it wasn't possible on the Ascari bend.*

Every effort was made to lighten each piece of the car, and it was continually returned to the factory to improve its performance. Finally, the number 48771 was engraved on the top surface of the left frame rail.

The second contender for the prize was the Bugatti team, led by Jean Bugatti, son of Ettore Bugatti. Jean-Pierre Wimille was to have been Bugatti's primary driver, but he was injured in a car accident on the way to the track. Although not as fast as his colleague, Robert Benoist filled in for Wimille and began practicing immediately. On August 23, Bugatti decided to make its attempt. Benoist did his best, but the press described his performance as "hesitant." He failed to qualify for the Million by 9.5 seconds, and the disappointed Bugatti team was forced to pin its hopes upon a recovering Jean-Pierre Wimille.

*Below: Écurie Bleue even used Delahaye support vehicles. Facing page: Lucy and Laury Schell arriving in Monaco driving a Delahaye Type 135 special on a short chassis.*

RALLYE AUTOMOBILE MON
ARRIVÉE
29 JANVIER 1936
707-RK
41
RALLYE MONTE-CARLO

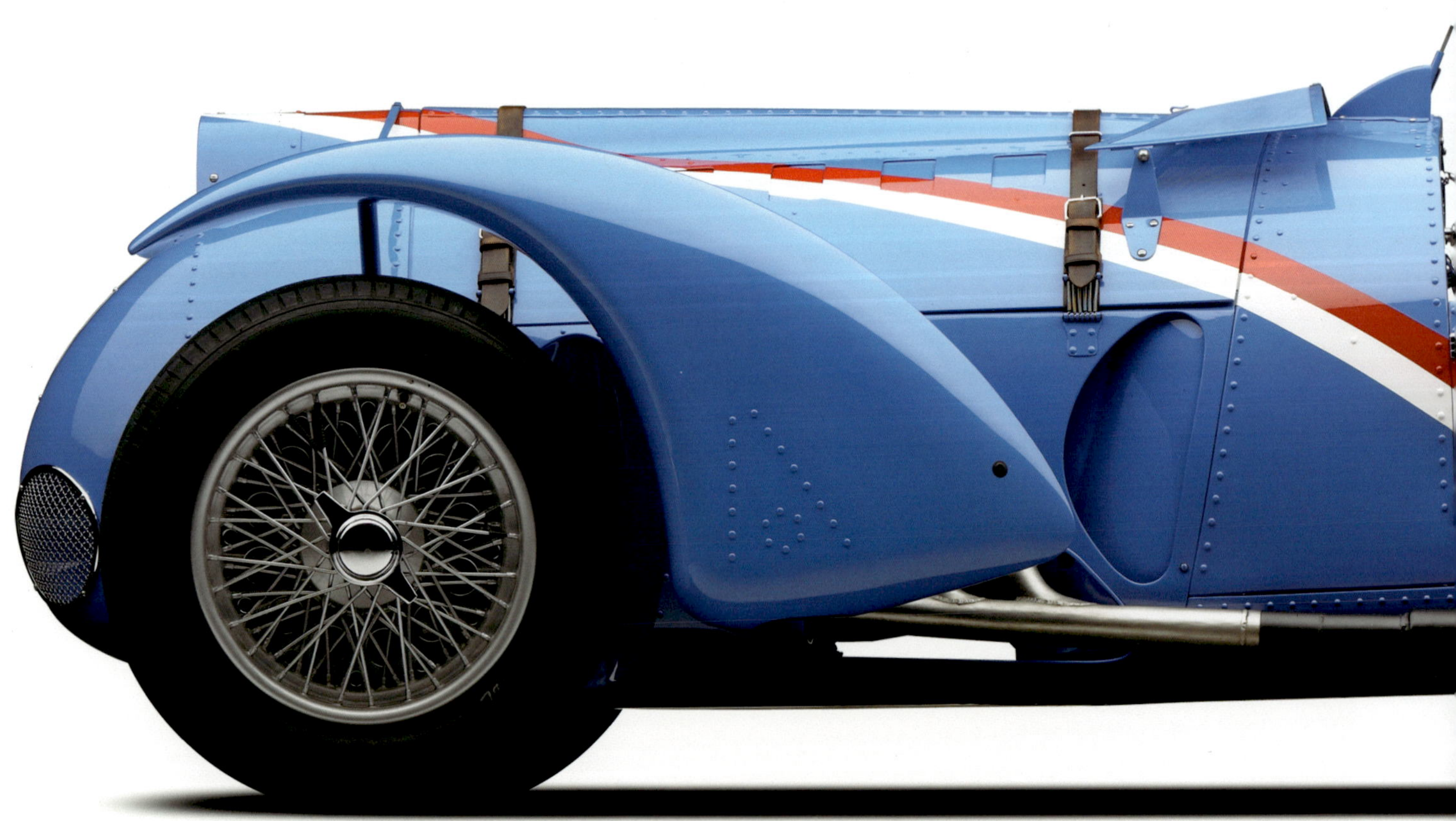

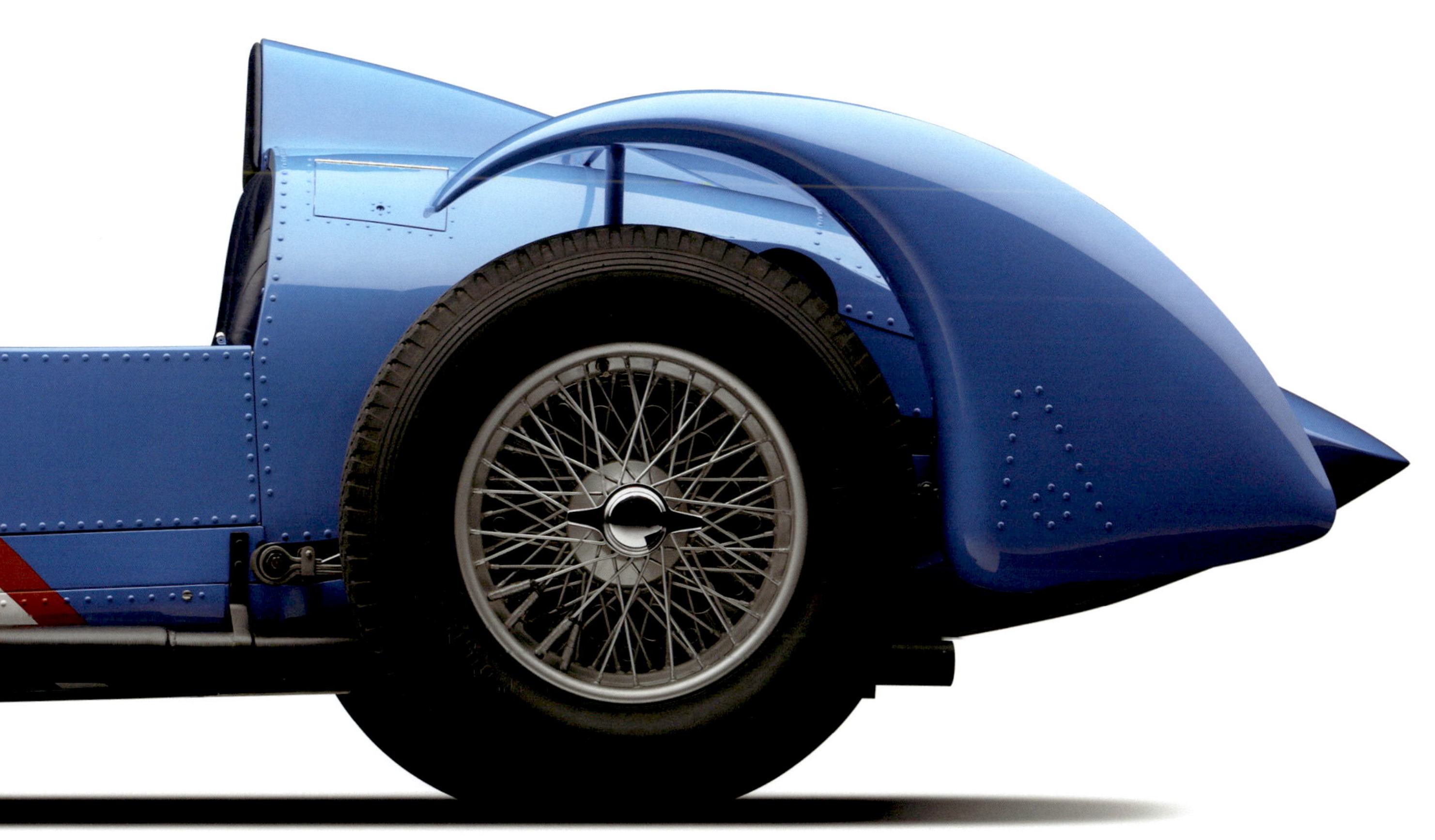

DELAHAYE

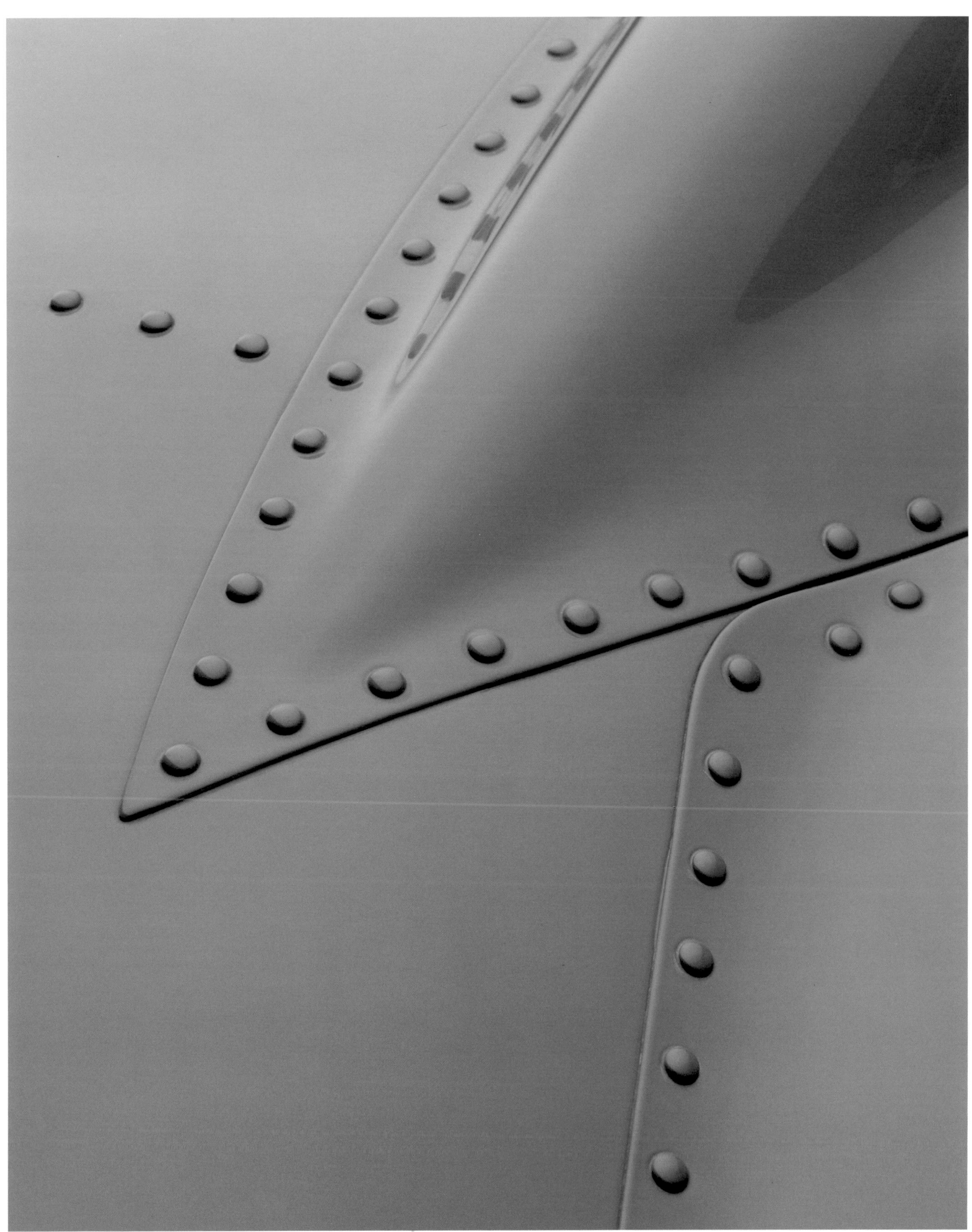

*Above: The body of this car was riveted together, making the shapes sculptural.*
*Facing page, top: The steering wheel is made of spring steel to absorb some of the road vibrations.*
*Facing page, bottom: The belt holding the hood down has springs, which allows the car's body to flex.*

In the meantime, Dreyfus was also hard at work each day at Montlhéry, but he was unhappy with his speed on the crucial first lap. He kept telling Weiffenbach that he wasn't ready for the final attempt. Monsieur Charles arrived on August 26 to convince his reluctant driver that he could win. Dreyfus was unmoved, claiming he needed more time to prepare. But Monsieur Charles had a trick up his sleeve, and when Dreyfus arrived at the track on the morning of August 27, he found that there would be no tests that day. Instead, in his words, "the whole press corps was at the track to watch my attempt to beat the record."

"To say that I was angry is an understatement," continued Dreyfus. "Normally I'm the gentlest man in the world. But Monsieur Charles had decided and the French press plus the foreign press were there, not to mention Jean François. The crowd had read about it in the morning papers, and would soon begin arriving." He was faced with a fait accompli.

Dreyfus was tense and refused to talk to anyone. The mechanics had worked all night on the car but at the scheduled 7 a.m. start time, it was still not sorted out. Finally, at 9 a.m., the ACF called to ask if Dreyfus was ready, and his response was to get into the car. According to Dreyfus, "I drove as I had never driven in my life." When he came in, he had broken the record at 1 hour 21 minutes 49 5/10 seconds, 146.654 km/hr. As of Friday, August 27, he had won the Million—for the moment.

Later that same day, Wimille arrived by airplane from Nice, still not recovered completely but determined to win. There were rumors that the Bugatti car would not compete, but Dreyfus had to be ready to take to the track immediately. "For four full days," he said, "we suffered. You had to consider, for instance, that a competitor might know he had more power than I had, and could attempt his performance at the last minute on August 31. This meant that I would have to start when dusk had fallen, which I preferred not to do. In any case, I was there constantly from morning till night." To address these fears, the Delahaye team spoke to the ACF the day before the deadline and was able to obtain permission to start two minutes after Bugatti, should driver Wimille begin his try around dusk.

*René Dreyfus on the track with his mechanics and members of the press prior to his attempt to win the Million Franc Prize.*

On Tuesday, August 31, Wimille finally started at 6:43 p.m., and Dreyfus followed two minutes later. Dreyfus drove like a tiger, surpassing the speed he'd achieved when he broke the record on August 27.

> *I had decided that if by chance Jean-Pierre broke down, I would stop, so that I could keep the record I'd set the week before, given the fact that it was not worth it at that hour to try and risk even more. Finally, at the end of seven or eight laps, I received the signal that I'd beaten the record of the week before. Then I found myself getting ahead of him in speed, although I had started later, and when I went past the pit, I saw Jean-Pierre's car stopped and some smoke around the pit. I think he'd had piston trouble. Nevertheless, suspecting that there still might be a little trick behind it all, I did not stop immediately. It was only two or three laps later that my wife and Monsieur Charles gave me the clear sign: "You did it, you have the record."*

The exuberant crowd surged onto the field, and it was all over. Bugatti had abandoned the attempt. The Million belonged to Delahaye, to the Écurie Bleue team of Lucy Schell, and to René Dreyfus. "I came up to Jean-Pierre," remembered Dreyfus, "and I shook his hand. Wimille congratulated me. 'The best man won,' he said, and then added with a smile, 'My turn next!'"

*René Dreyfus getting a kiss from his wife, Chou-Chou.*

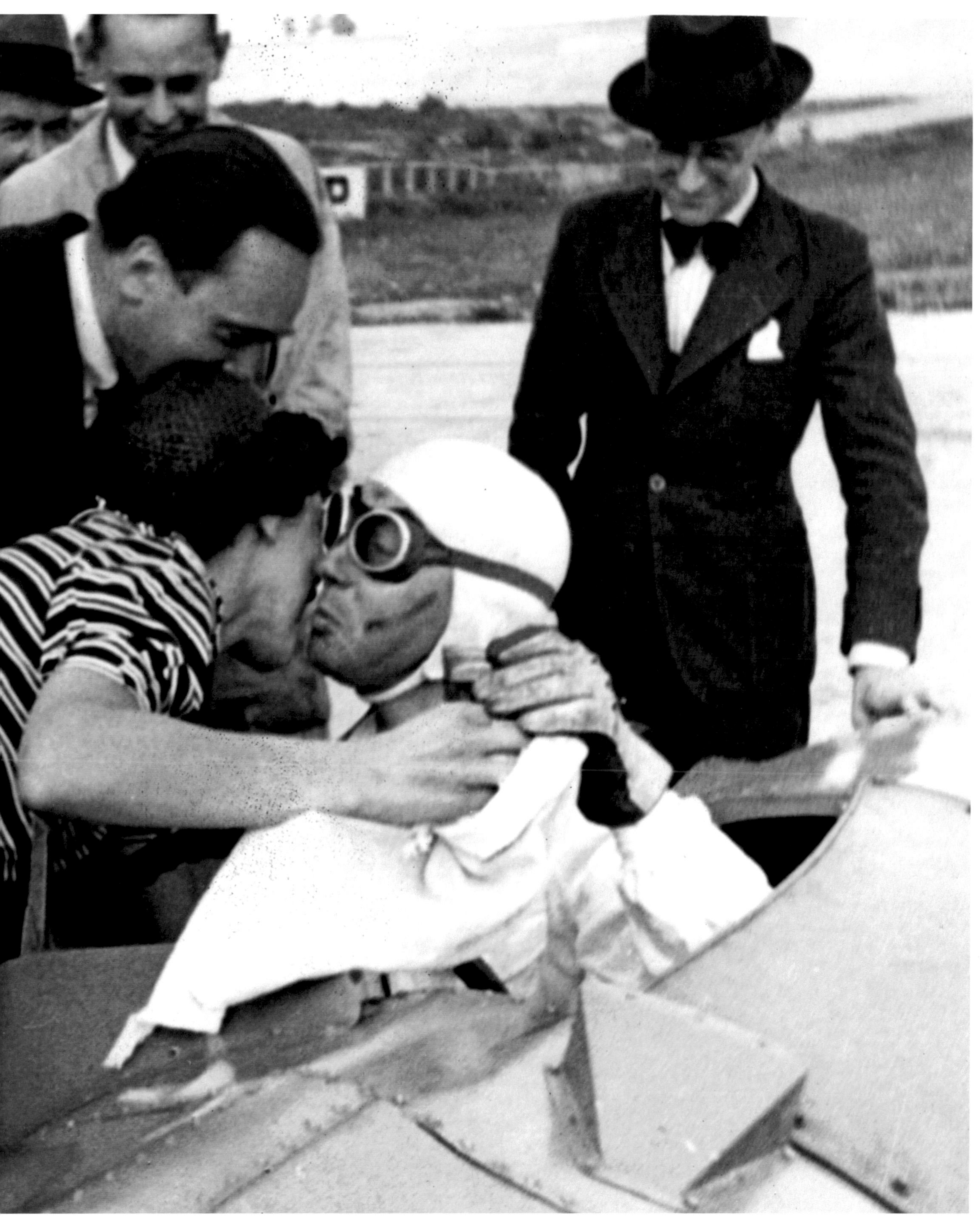

DELAHAYE

After its famous victory, Chassis 48771 went on to race again. However, before it next competed (in the 1939 Mille Miglia), it was rebodied with a faired-in headrest and cycle fenders that were teardrop shaped and individually enclosed to reduce drag. Just before World War II hostilities began, Lucy Schell sent all her Delahaye race cars back to the factory. The factory then realized it had a valuable object on its hands: one of the last Type 155 V-12 engines in magnesium, the rest having been scrapped for the war effort. Delahaye carefully kept it hidden and in 1947, after the war was over, decided to donate the engine and a transmission to Mr. André St. Blancard, the director of the Lycée Pilote de Montgeron, who was also in charge of training the apprentices at the Delahaye factory. They practiced their skills as mechanics by taking apart engines and bodies. The magnesium engine was to re-emerge many years later in surprising circumstances connected with Chassis 48771.

In 1948, Chassis 48771 was acquired by Charles Pozzi, French driver and entrepreneur, who intended to incorporate it into his racing team, the Écurie Lutétia. Since the chassis had no engine, Delahaye lent Pozzi its new Type 175 S engine. Pozzi entered the car in the Le Mans 24-hour race of 1949, but it was forced to retire in the eighth lap. It was then entered at the 1949 Grand Prix de l'ACF at Comminges, where it came in first. After 1950, when Delahaye stopped supporting its Type 175 S racing motor, Pozzi returned the engine to the factory, added a Ford Comète body to the racing chassis, and replaced the V-12 engine with a 3.5-liter, 6-cylinder Type 135 S engine. The body was an exact fit for the chassis and few modifications were required. After the 1951 season, Pozzi asked Jean-Pierre Bernard to sell the car.

Bernard was finally able to sell Chassis 48771 to collector Serge Pozzoli, who discarded the Ford Comète body and Type 135 S engine, and replaced the latter with the Type 155 V-12 magnesium engine and transmission that had been given to Blancard. However, Pozzoli and Bernard were unaware that this was the magnesium engine, believing it to be a Type 145. Pozzoli also recovered the body panels that Pozzi had preserved from the original V-12 body. Pozzoli stored the Delahaye for a long time under the stands at the Montlhéry racetrack, until he moved it to his Chateau du Gérier near Evreux, where he kept a huge collection of cars and bikes and one of the world's finest archives of automotive books. Several years later, when it was no longer competitive, Chassis 48771 was exhibited at Pozzoli's chateau, which was also a museum.

Few recalled the car's glorious past until Peter Mullin recognized and purchased it in 1987. With the help of French historian Philippe Bavouzet, Mr. Mullin obtained records from the Department of Mines, confirming that the car had been the winner of the Million Franc Prize. Chassis 48771 was sent to England for restoration by Crosthwaite and Gardiner, where the engine was rebuilt and the original racing body recreated. The coachwork followed the lines of the 1938 Delahaye entry in the Mille Miglia while retaining the original rear end and body panels. The engine didn't run very well even after its restoration, which, given that it had been repaired according to the wrong specifications, was entirely understandable. Finally in 2006, Jim Stranberg of High Mountain Classics reviewed the drawings for the Type 145, 155, and 165 engines. To his surprise, he found that the engine in Chassis 48771 was in fact a Type 155 V-12 magnesium engine, not a Type 145 as previously believed. None of the V-12 magnesium engines had been thought to have survived the war, and the single Type 155 race car that had been built had been considered lost for the last fifty years. The rediscovery of that car's engine came as a delightful surprise. Once the mechanics restored the engine using the correct information, the V-12 ran like a dream. For lovers of such historic cars, it is lucky that documents detailing these engines still exist.

All four Écurie Bleue Type 145s have square-splined hubs; the mounts for their cycle fenders are welded to the chassis, typical of race cars; and each car has a racing front suspension. Only Chassis 48771, however, has additional chassis modifications, indicating the exceptional effort that was made to reduce its weight and increase its speed. Its front spindles are hollow; the steel spring shackle bolts are lightened; the gas, brake, and clutch pedal assembly is drilled with holes to reduce its weight; and the rear axle is hollow. The manual transmission housing is magnesium, which was more expensive but lighter than aluminum.

*Chassis 48771 when it was owned by Serge Pozzoli; some of the parts and the front bodywork were missing. After hearing about the car at Rétromobile in 1987, Jim Hull and Peter Mullin purchased the Delahaye.*

The remaining Type 145s went on to lead colorful lives. Two, Chassis 48772 and Chassis 48773, were mistaken for each other for some time, giving experts much to discuss. In light of the extensive opinions bandied about, it is remarkable that a detailed, hands-on examination of the cars in question was not performed sooner. When this was at last done, it shed light on what could have caused the mix up so long ago. The hypothesis is that when the two Delahaye coupés were present simultaneously at Henri Chapron's coach-building shop, either their chassis frames or their records might have been switched. This would mean that the documents that followed the cars through the years included identifying numbers that did not match the actual numbers stamped on various parts of the cars.

When disassembled by Jim Stranberg in 2006, the chassis identified as 48772 was found to have that number stamped on the frame rail. However, the Delahaye chassis plate on the firewall was stamped with 48773, and the Chapron coachbuilder plaque on the firewall was stamped with Chapron order number 6517, as were many of the car's other parts. The documents that accompanied the car stated that Chapron order number 6517 corresponded to Chassis 48773, so it became clear that something was awry.

In the case of the car identified on page 111 as Chassis 48773, Mr. Stranberg looked in vain for a chassis number on the frame rails, but he did find Chapron order number 6351 stamped on many of its parts. The car's chassis plate and the Chapron coach-builder plaque normally placed upon the firewall were lost during restoration in Germany. The documents for the car stated that Chapron order number 6351 corresponded to Chassis 48772.

The conclusion is that Chassis 48772 corresponds to Chapron order number 6517, and in the absence of a chassis number on the frame rails of the other car, the assumption is that Chapron order number 6351 corresponds to Chassis 48773. Both cars are now part of the Mullin Collection, and this book describes their histories in detail. Why this confusion first came about is impossible to establish for certain, but it should be pointed out that in decades past, a chassis number was less important than at present, especially when the car in question is a classic Delahaye. In days gone by, a chassis was often rebodied several times, especially when it was constantly being updated to race at different venues, and far more importance was given to the coachwork that sat on top of the chassis. It is only in recent years that the chassis and its number have become crucial historical identifiers that prevent fraud or misrepresentation and allow careful stewards to maintain accurate data concerning the provenance of their cars.

Chassis 48772 was produced in 1938 and was bought by Henri Chapron from the Écurie Bleue team after it was finished with its racing career. In January 1947 he removed the race car coachwork and began to rebody the car as a two-place coupé for Robert Cuny, manager of Modern Transports in Vosges, France.

*Early portrait of Henri Chapron.*

*Facing page: The Grand Prix de l'ACF at Reims, France, on July 9, 1939. The car in the foreground, believed to be Chassis 48772, was part of the Écurie Bleue team and finished in 9th place.*

*1937 Delahaye 145 Coupé - Chassis No. 48772*

A great deal of correspondence was exchanged between Cuny and Chapron concerning the details of the car, which was promised for delivery in six months. By August 1947, however, Chapron was explaining that production had been interrupted by strikes and labor problems, followed by the annual summer holiday period. In December, Cuny was busy selecting finishes and paint color. The car was eventually delivered in March 1948, painted custom Chapron blue and sporting gray seats of pleated leather. Under the hood it had a Type 165 V-12 engine (stamped number 6), three Solex carburetors left-over from its racing career, single-plug heads, a standard Type 165 block, and front and rear suspension (not Type 145 suspension as previously thought). The mechanical work to repair and tune up the engine was entrusted to Delahaye expert Fernand Lacour of the Wilson Garage, who was also involved with Chassis 48773.

Mr. Cuny showed off his car at the Rallye de Lorraine to much acclaim. He consigned the car a few years later to Jean-Pierre Bernard, who was managing the Delahaye showroom at the time. From there it was sold to an unknown official at the Supreme Headquarters of the Allied Powers in Europe (SHAPE). At some point it was painted racing green, and the V-12 motor was replaced by a competition Type 135 S engine. The car was later bought by the Schlumpf brothers, owners of a private car collection in Mulhouse, France. During the brothers' ownership, it is believed that a 6-cylinder Type 135 unit was installed in the car. The Schlumpfs kept Chassis 48772 for many years until they sold it to Ed Andrews of Chicago for $3,000 via the brokerage services of A.F. Loyens of Luxembourg. Andrews shipped it off to Chicago during a winter when the waterway into Lake Huron was frozen, so the Delahaye was taken off the ship in Detroit, and Andrews and his brother filled up the tank and drove it to Chicago.

*1938-46 Delahaye 145 Coupé - Chassis No. 48773*

Through a stroke of good fortune, in 1970 Andrews was able to buy the original V-12 engine from Loyens for $5,000. Loyens had apparently acquired this engine from a French collector who had kept it on an engine stand for display. After making the purchase, Andrews stored the engine in Chicago in several boxes.

In 1972, Andrews took the Delahaye to Hal and Bill Ullrich's Chicago shop for restoration, where it remained for eight years. From there it was sent to Frank Opalka's shop in Evanston, Illinois, but apparently after such a long interval, Andrews had become discouraged and preferred to focus on his Bugatti. In the end, the car was sold to car dealer Bill Jacobs, Jr.

Strother MacMinn, car design expert and professor at the Art Center in Pasadena, California, wrote a long article entitled "Delahaye Type 145 Coupé by Henri Chapron" detailing the restoration of this car, from which the following excerpt is taken:

*Persistent and dedicated enthusiasm is the main reason that many of the great cars of yesterday are still with us. Fortunately, that lifeline lasted through a whole generation of indifference until prices and profit went up high enough to make restoration a logical pastime. It was genuine enthusiasm that moved Bill Hinds of Monterey, California, to locate, restore and drive a series of Delahayes. Luckily, he was able to share this enchantment with Bill Jacobs, Jr., a Chicago Chevrolet/BMW dealer and avid enthusiast. When Hinds began to extol the virtues of a 12-cylinder Type 165 hidden somewhere in the Chicago area it took Jacobs just one day to locate Andrews and his hidden treasure, and a little longer to persuade him to sell it. This was in the very beginning of 1983 and the car was promptly sent out to Monterey so that a full restoration could be started immediately.*

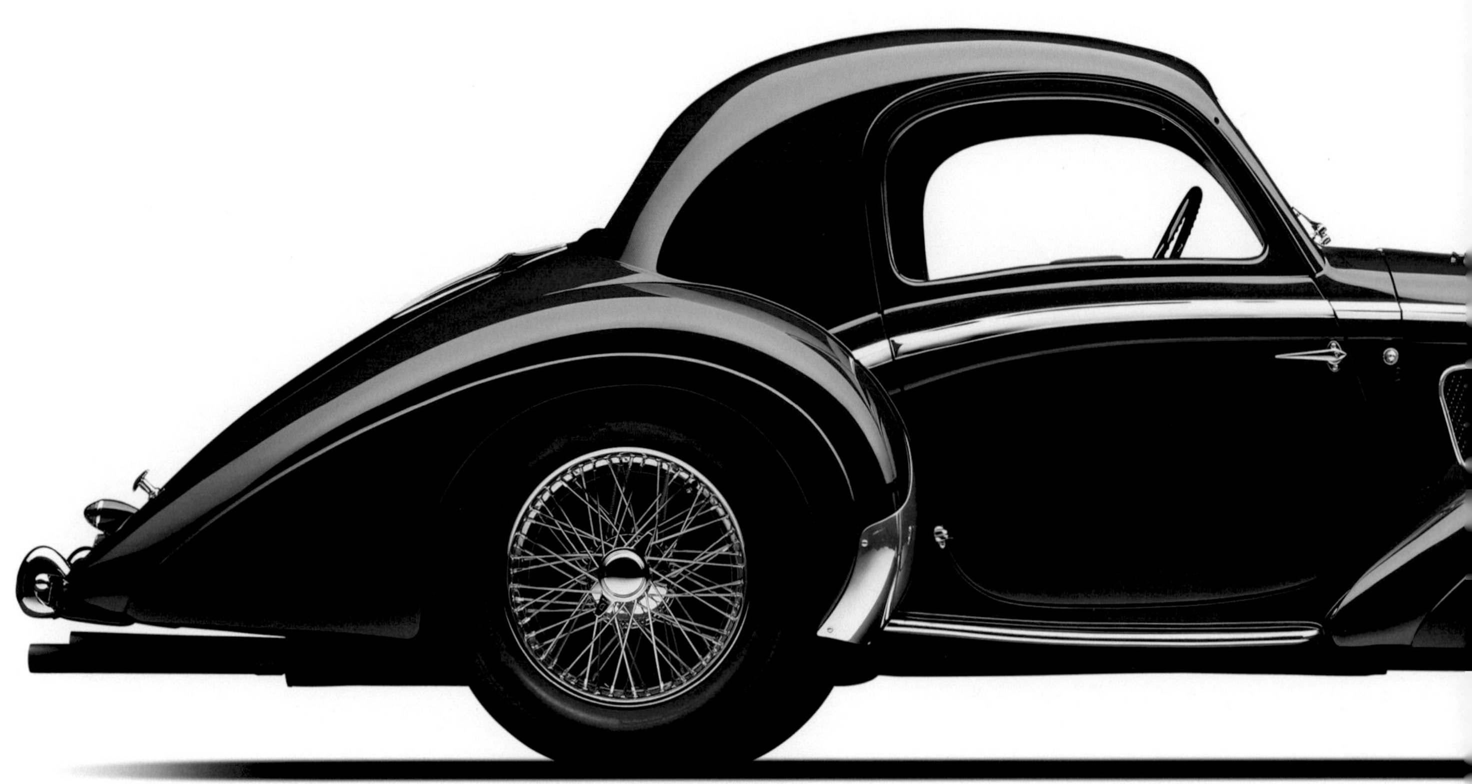

*The priceless 12-cylinder engine (No. 6), disassembled and in boxes, was turned over to Alec Giamo, master engine builder in Redwood City, fifty miles north of Monterey. As he studied the parts, began assembly, and communicated with Jacobs in Chicago and with Hinds, it became apparent that this was actually a racing engine that had been detuned to make it tractable (as opposed to an engine that had been specifically built for grand touring). The triple carburetor manifold with its American Stromberg EE3s, the multiple plate clutch and flywheel assembly, lightweight timing gears, solid lifters and lightweight valve mechanism, and special crankshaft counterweights for high rpm operation were all intended for serious competition performance. Simultaneously, down in Monterey, Hinds discovered enough evidence, including the original fender bracket mounts, French racing blue paint, rigid engine mounts, and racing welds, to confirm that this chassis had indeed been a competition racer. When Giamo completed the engine he put it on a dynamometer to tune and test it and succeeded in pulling 184.18 bhp at 4,000 rpm, and also recorded 221 lbs/ft of torque at the same rate which compares well with the original ratings.*

"A very great deal of this particular car's beauty comes from its color scheme that reveals and complements the form," writes MacMinn about the coachwork.

*Bill Jacobs said that he knew from the beginning what colors he wanted to use on the car but it also must be said that his superb taste and empathy interpreting this scheme is also responsible for the extraordinarily beautiful result. Henri Chapron's skill in using raised panels to define the areas for a second or accent color was legendary. Most designers of the period confined this treatment to the beltline that runs from the radiator shell back to the cowl, under the windows, and on down the edge of the rear deck or across the back of the body. As previously mentioned, Chapron additionally embossed a panel on the sides of the fenders that paralleled their profiles and thus emphasized their curve while visually reducing their mass. A navy blue was chosen for the base color and was complemented by a deep, burgundy red for the accents, the two colors being almost the same in value (or darkness). For a final touch, both colors were applied using what is called a "French lacquer" technique in which barely a thimbleful of iridescence is added to one of the clear coats over the base color. The result is the most subtle softening of the highlights with a pearlescent trail that adds an incredible richness to the color in direct light. The transformation of the car as it moves from shade into sunlight has to be seen to be fully appreciated.*

The Delahaye re-emerged in September 1984, and Bill Jacobs exhibited his car at the Blackhawk Concours in San Ramon, California, and in 1985 at the Pebble Beach Concours d'Élégance. Blackhawk later purchased the car and sold it to Samuel Orenstein, who in turn sold it to Myron Schuster. It was restored in 1993, and in 2003 it was purchased by the Mullin Collection, restored to its original Chapron configuration, and shown in 2006 at the Pebble Beach Concours d'Élégance.

*Facing page: 1937 Delahaye 145 Coupé - Chassis No. 48772.*

We now pick up the history of Chassis 48773 (Chapron order number 6351), long mistaken for Chassis 48772. It is believed to have been produced in 1938 as one of the four sold to Lucy and Laury Schell for their new Type 145 racing team. Records show that an A.M. Duprie bought the chassis in 1939 from the Schells' son, Harry, himself an amateur racer. At some point after that, Duprie took the car to Chapron and work was started on the body. Everything came to a halt with the beginning of World War II, and the car was left unfinished in the shop. At the end of the war, Chapron was unable to locate Duprie, who had disappeared without paying for the work that had been done. Chassis 48773 and the unfinished body were impounded by Nothomb Impoundment, which represented the local French government. In September 1945 it was bought for 350,000 French francs by J. Vanpoucque, who was assisted in the purchase by the same Fernand Lacour involved with Chassis 48772. Chapron started to finish Vanpoucque's sports coupé (Chapron order number 6351), but the two men's correspondence makes it evident that difficulties soon arose. First there is a letter dated May 1947 wherein Vanpoucque inquires anxiously about the state of his car. Then there are a number of increasingly testy replies from Chapron, complaining that he has not been paid and threatening to remove the coachwork and keep the bare chassis. In the end, a lien was placed on the car by the Office of Economic Recovery (Office de Récupération Économique, or O.R.E.), but the vehicle remained at the Chapron shop. In May 1948, the O.R.E. wrote to Chapron requesting that he make the car available to prospective buyers, and asking him to provide a list of his expenses. Chapron replied in June, offering to buy the car for 100,000 French francs, which apparently was not enough. On December 28, 1950, Chapron wrote to Auguste Veuillet, accepting his offer to buy the coachwork for 600,000 French francs, with the understanding that Veuillet would make his own arrangements with Lacour regarding the chassis and engine. By December 30, 1950, the parties had agreed to the conditions of the sale and Veuillet's company, Sonauto, had promised to pay by January 10, 1951. The car's registration was changed from 31RS3 to 938R75. That same year, Sonauto sold the car to Max Hoffmann, the United States importer of BMWs, and shipped it to New York. It changed hands once more in 1951 when it was bought by William Procter of Green Farms, Connecticut.

According to Chris Laidlaw's interview with Lew Gotthainer, which appeared in *Motorsport*, Procter "drove it for six months. It started losing a lot of oil, so he took it to Zumbach, a foreign car shop in New York City, who said the trouble was that the engine had had a lot of wear—not surprising when you remember that it had been raced about ten years before. Procter tried to sue Hoffman, but got nowhere. He got fed up with the car and sold it to Robert Grier." Grier then had the engine completely rebuilt.

"The engine work was done," says Laidlaw, "but the engine had not been put back in the car when he took it to Austin Clark's Museum to sit for a short while, which turned out to be 20 years."

*Bob Grier, René Dreyfus, and Chassis 48773 at René Dreyfus's restaurant, Le Chanteclair, in New York City. The spot was the unofficial meeting place for international race car drivers.*

In June 1971, Gotthainer and his wife were in France and were interviewed by Henri Chapron and Jean-Pierre Bernard. "One day in 1970 when I was visiting Austin Clark's Museum," said Mr. Gotthainer:

> *I stopped dead in front of a 12-cylinder Delahaye motor in one of the corridors of the museum. It turned out to be the unfinished engine of Chassis 60744, sent to the United States for the French Exhibit of the New York World's Fair of 1939. Austin said he had another car to show me. It was parked haphazardly, in the back of the museum, where to judge from the tarp covering the chassis, the pigeons were nesting. It belonged to the widow of Bob Grier, a rich New Yorker who was friends with race driver René Dreyfus, and also passionate about French cars. He'd placed it in Clark's museum because the problems with his business made him believe that it could be confiscated for unpaid taxes. His death occurred before restoration was complete. I did not know, therefore, if we were dealing with a re-bodied race car or something else. Its aesthetics delighted me, especially its long hood which ended almost at the center of the car. It also had a convertible roof driven by a clever gear system, powered by an electric motor. So Clark put me in touch with Mrs. Grier, from whom I bought the car and the second engine.*
>
> *I took it to Hibernia Restorations, because I had had good reports from Fahnestock, who'd sent them his Type 165, the ex-Adrian Conan Doyle car (Chassis 60743). Once the restoration was finished, my Delahaye 145 was then repainted in blue gray, just as it was originally, and at that point I really came to discover the car. It was superb, with pure lines and not a single lapse in taste. Because I admired the design and was interested in the history of my car, I came to Paris to meet with Mr. Henri Chapron... It was then that I learned that we were dealing with one of the race cars used, among others, by René Dreyfus.*

*Chassis 48773 at an early driving event on an airport tarmac in the New York area.*

# Motorsport

OCTOBER
25¢
K

HOT RODS · SPORT CARS · STOCK CARS · RACE CARS · ANTIQUE CAR

Gotthainer later met Uwe Hucke, who bought the unfinished Delahaye engine from him. Then in 1972, finding that he had a few too many automobiles in his collection, Gotthainer sold the car itself to Hucke, who shipped it to France. In 1977, it was bought by Count Hubertus von Doenhoff along with the unfinished Delahaye engine. In the early 1990s Peter Mullin, who had known of and admired the car for many years, visited the Count in an attempt to purchase it, although he was unsuccessful at that time. However in 2004, it was displayed at Rétromobile in Paris and sold to the Mullin Collection.

The last of the four Type 145s produced for the Million Franc Prize, and the second to be ordered by the Écurie Bleue, was Chassis 48772-3. It was campaigned in many races, and it remains special today as the only one of the four existing cars with a Type 145 engine (stamped "1") and an aluminum block. Of the other three, two had Type 165 engines and the third had a Type 155 engine.

These Type 145s were essential components of the Écurie Bleue team. Sadly, Laury Schell was killed in an accident just before the start of World War II. His son, Harry, left France for the United States and took with him two Maseratis that were entered in the 1940 Indianapolis 500. The drivers were René Le Bègue and René Dreyfus, the latter having been released by the French Army so that he could represent his country. The invasion of France took place in 1940, and because of Germany's treatment of the Jews, Dreyfus was warned not to return. He remained in New York and became a successful restaurateur.

Once the war began, racing throughout Europe came to a halt. It picked up again in 1945, but few new cars were built and those raced were mostly models created before the war. One exception was the Delahaye Type 175 S, which had a brief racing career. But the Delahaye company was unable to insert new capital into a racing program and could no longer count on the deep pockets of the Écurie Bleue, which had ceased to exist with the death of Laury. When the new wave of post-war cars began, Delahaye could no longer compete.

*Facing page: William Procter's Delahaye Type 145, Chassis 48773, on the October 1951 cover of* Motorsport.

# DELAGE

# DELAGE

# THE DELAGE COMPANY

The company that created *La Belle Voiture Française*, or "The Beautiful French Car," opened for business in 1905 and ended its distinguished contribution to France's auto industry in 1953. The founder of the Delage company was Louis Delage, born in Cognac in 1874 and, like Émile Delahaye, a graduate of the prestigious École Nationale Supérieure d'Arts et Métiers at Angers. After graduating in 1893, Delage completed his military service and then left for Paris, the hub of the French automobile industry and a world center of art and design. In 1900 he briefly set up shop as a consulting engineer and then joined Peugeot in 1903. Those were early days for Peugeot, which had just transitioned from bicycles to cars, and the company provided an excellent environment for Delage to learn his craft. He was eventually promoted to tests and studies manager before leaving, in 1905, to start his own company. To do so, he obtained modest financial backing from Alfred Baudier and recruited a colleague, Augustin Legros, a skilled engineer with whom he had worked at Peugeot. The decision to do so was typical of Delage, who always had a particular knack for picking top talents. Legros became Delage's second in command, and although they often fought, disagreed, argued, and occasionally parted ways, they went on to design and produce great cars for thirty-one years.

Legros and Delage started work in a small shop in the area of Levallois, just northwest of Paris, where they developed two prototypes for the Paris Auto Salon of December 1905, although they had already had some sales success since joining forces in August. These prototypes were 1-cylinder *voiturettes* with De Dion Bouton engines, and the public and press received the cars with enthusiasm. Delage was a passionate fan of racing and quickly understood the effect a successful race car could have on his marketing. A year later he entered the Coupe des Voiturettes de l'Auto in Paris. The 1906 event, which took place in driving rain and mud, was a series of races over five days (November 5 to 11). A Sizaire et Naudin eventually prevailed; one

*Facing page: Delage sales brochure advertising the Type D8-120.*

Delage crashed into a tree, but another placed second, beating the Peugeot. As a result, Delage won a gold medal and received 30 percent of the proceeds taken at the race. When the fledgling business appeared at the 1906 Paris Auto Salon, orders poured in and the company was able to become a serious player in the business.

The Delage team entered the same race in 1907, but the competition had developed more horsepower for their motors and was not to be beaten so easily. Seventh place was the best the Delage racers could manage, so Louis Delage decided to develop and build his own engine for the next season. With a great deal of difficulty and borrowing from motorcycle technology, the company produced a sophisticated 1-cylinder, 100-mm bore, high-compression engine with four valves and four spark plugs. The engine was dubbed the Causan in honor of Némorin Causan, the engineer who designed it, and it was placed on a new chassis for the 1908 Grand Prix des Voiturettes,a very popular race featuring small and affordable models. Delage entered three Causans, which came in first, fifth, and twelfth. "The victory of Delage," wrote *Omnia* magazine "delighted all the spectators. Its excellent construction hadn't guaranteed any miracles, but it did produce them." The results of this race had a strong effect on the company's sales and established the marque's solid reputation in the auto industry.

A breakthrough year for Delage was 1910. He hired Arthur Michelat, another graduate of the Arts et Métiers schools, as chief product designer and engineer, while Legros became plant and marketing manager. The team was later joined by engineer Maurice Gaultier, who became responsible for the production of Delage touring cars. This freed up Michelat to concentrate on the racing department, and he was able to design a new and more powerful race car for the 1911 season. The Delage Type X contained one of the very first twin camshaft, 3-liter, 4-cylinder motors. On June 25, 1911, in the Coupe de l'Auto—one of the most-watched races in France—the Delage Type X race cars came in first, third, and fourth in a very close competition. The excitement and interest this feat created among the public convinced Delage to build bigger, stronger models, and to drop his 1-cylinder cars and 4-cylinder Ballot engines. As a result, the factory expanded to a larger location at Boulevard de Courbevoie, and in 1912 the AH model, a Delage-designed 6-cylinder, 2.5-liter, 14 hp engine, emerged from the production line.

Once World War I started in 1914, the company devoted itself to the war effort, producing ammunition, trucks, and cars for the military. Remarkably, the company managed to continue developing new cars for the French Army, although most were actually 1914 models modified for military purposes. These cars included

*Facing page: "If you're going to do just one thing, do it well."*
*- Louis Delage*

La six cylindres
Delâge
et ses freins avant

"Ne faire qu'une chose,
Mais la bien faire"

L. Delâge.

140. avenue Champs Elysées
Paris

the Type BI (civilian Type AI) and the new 6-cylinder Type BK (civilian Type AK), both of which premiered in December 1915. The Type CO however, which became available the following year, was a genuinely new article. It had 6 cylinders, twin carburetors, and a 6-seat touring body. Although a second series Type CO was later sold to the public after being introduced at the 1919 Paris Auto Salon, the military Type CO, or CO "E," was built primarily to meet the French Army's needs.

By the end of the war, Louis Delage was a very wealthy man. He believed in living life at full bore on the track and beyond, and he spent his riches on an elegant house on the Avenue Foch by the Bois de Boulogne, on the Chateau de St Germain in Le Pecq in the posh Paris suburbs, and on La Campanella, his villa in St. Briac in Brittany. Although Delage was a genuine lover of the sea who enjoyed simple pastimes with his parents and family, he was also famous for flamboyant entertaining, sometimes hosting five hundred guests at a time at his villa or on one of his new yachts, the Vieille Chose I and the Vieille Chose II. In addition, he bought a lavish house on the Champs-Élysées that he turned into a fashionable showroom. It was from there that he launched his Grand Touring luxury cars, which the public proclaimed *La Belle Voiture Française*. Meanwhile, France was suffering from rampant inflation because of the aftereffects of World War I, so sales were slow at first, but better results came with the Type DE created for the 1921 Paris Auto Salon. As soon as the car appeared, it received a rave review in the November 1922 issue of *Omnia* magazine: "Because of its simplicity, the arrangement of its components and their correct proportions, its strong construction and its perfect road holding, it fully justifies its success." To promote its new model, the Delage company sent Pierre Delage, Louis's son, to drive the standard touring version of the Type DE, without racing modifications, on a promotional endurance run. This trip around France took place in September 1921 over the course of fifteen days, during which time the car and its occupants visited every primary Delage agent in France. The journey covered a total of 8575 km and took place without mishap.

*The Delage factory in Courbevoie, a commune in Paris, prior to being purchased by Delahaye in 1935.*

*The Delage showroom on the Champs-Élysées in the late 1920s.*

One year later, a driver named Bequet made a second promotional run, this time from Paris to Madrid. The car arrived at its destination in twenty hours and thirty minutes, covering an amazing 1380 km on primitive roads. After this extraordinary accomplishment and several other endurance contests that were promoted by various media, the Type DE was displayed at the Delage company's showroom on the Champs-Élysées in honor of its achievements. The model became a favorite of the public because of its style, reliability, and high quality. It was also reasonably priced for the period, selling at 29,550 French francs, including coachwork, and during those difficult economic times the profits from the Delage Type DE were very welcome. An article in the September 25, 1922, issue of *La Vie Automobile* said, "the 11 hp Delage is one of the most successful realizations of a medium power car suitable for all purposes...a very high class car."

The Type DE line sold well during 1922, but then sales dropped and inventory piled up. In 1923 the company reorganized its corporate structure and went public. Rather than using the funds from the share sales to retool the factory, Louis Delage decided to build a "super car," the Type GL. This was Delage's first foray into the luxury car market, and he spared no expense: he used his windfall profits from the manufacture of shells during World War I to create a vehicle that was to compete against Hispano-Suiza and surpass Rolls-Royce, the latter of which was promoted in the English press as the "Best Car in the World." The bare Type GL chassis was first revealed at the 1924 Paris Auto Salon with an asking price of 85,000 French francs. The French press received the car with great enthusiasm but unfortunately, when the model became available in 1924, it sold only 180 units because of its high cost, which the recovering European economy could not afford. The Type GL passenger model was, however, an excellent car, with a sophisticated and state-of-the-art design. Although it did not sell as well as other high-class models of the time, the car was not in any way a failure—in the long run, its sales record was matched only by the Hispano-Suiza H6. Its introduction was also an important technical milestone for Delage, as the car featured an all-new straight 6-cylinder alloy engine, a single or dual overhead camshaft, and a single down-draft carburetor.

On the racetrack, the company took a new approach. In the early 1920s, Delage developed three cars for hill climbs and sprints. The first was the Type DF, which appeared at Marseille in April 1922; it was based on the 6-cylinder Type CO2 and won every hill climb it entered. Then newly recruited racing engineer Charles Planchon created the 12-cylinder, twin overhead camshaft Type DH, which set a new land speed record on July 6, 1924. In 1925 the last of the three cars, the Type DJ, appeared. It was based on the Type GL Grand Sport model and had a powerful 8-liter engine with twin overhead camshafts.

After this and other successes in competitive racing events, Planchon was charged with creating a new engine that would comply with the new rules of the ACF. He developed what would become his finest work:

*1939 Delage D8-120 with Chapron cabriolet coachwork.*

the 2LCV, a 2-liter, dual overhead camshaft V-12 motor, rumored to have been built in only ninety days. The car with the 2LCV first appeared at the Grand Prix de l'ACF in 1923, but it arrived late and did not have time to practice. As a result, it was not properly sorted out and broke down in the sixth lap. Delage flew into one of his famous rages and Planchon was fired. Turning to Albert Lory, who would become the company's chief engineer, Delage instructed him to make the engine work. Lory was successful and after that, the car achieved a good record of success during the 1924 and 1925 seasons, winning several races and achieving many podium finishes.

In 1926, the French economy plunged further into crisis. Delage could no longer obtain credit from his bankers, and inventory piled up to the point that unsold cars were parked in every available corner of the plant. Nevertheless, Delage kept moving ahead, seeming to thrive in moments of emergency.

The ACF changed the rules again for the 1926 season, requiring a new motor with a maximum capacity of 1.5 liters. Having anticipated this alteration, Lory had already begun developing a 1.5-liter version of the fabulous 2-liter V-12 engine. But this version did not prove entirely satisfactory, so the technology of the V-12 was used to create a straight-eight motor. The final product became a legend in racing history: a straight-eight, 1.5-liter, supercharged, dual overhead camshaft engine renowned for its mechanical sophistication and reliability. The car with this engine put in a good performance for the 1926 season: third place at the Grand Prix of Europe, third place at the Grand Prix of Spain, and first and third place at the British Grand Prix.

In 1927, Louis Delage finally won the World Construction Championship. With Robert Benoist driving, a Delage came in first in the Grand Prix de l'Ouverture, first in the Grand Prix de l'ACF, first in the

*1939 Delage D8-120 S with Letourneur & Marchand aerosport coachwork.*

Grand Prix of Spain, first in the Grand Prix of Europe, and first, second, and third in the British Grand Prix. Unfortunately, despite this triumph, the company was headed for rough financial waters. Commercial and marketing mistakes meant that the assets of the racing team had to be sold to private entrants, who continued to campaign the cars until the 1950s, although they had no financial support from the factory. In 1936, the success of these private entries led to the creation of two racing chassis for the Delage Type 1500, the World Championship model. Of those two chassis, one was purchased by collector Rob Walker in the 1950s. That car eventually became the Delage ERA, which is part of the Mullin Collection.

After winning the World Construction Championship in 1927 and earning the Légion d'Honneur (the highest decoration in France, established by Napoleon), Delage was forced to face financial reality and a changed marketplace. The Americans were selling their cars aggressively in Europe at reasonable prices, cars that were complete, including both chassis and coachwork. Citroën and Renault were following suit, but rather than move with the times, Delage continued to use separate coachbuilders to body its chassis, opting to abandon race car production and focus exclusively on luxury chassis. The outcome was the Type DR, a new model for the 1927 Paris Auto Salon, also designed to compete head-to-head with Hispano-Suiza and Rolls-Royce. It was followed in September of 1929 by the Type D8, which premiered at the Paris Auto Salon in October of that year. The Type D8 marked the start of the marque's brilliant appearances at many concours d'élégance. Its powerful straight-eight motor and excellent chassis attracted the best coachbuilders, and it became an immediate success in the high-end market, winning many major awards at the concours

"La Belle Voiture Française"

l'appelation, si flatteuse pour nous, par laquelle le public synthétise nos voitures, nous crée d'années en années, l'impérieux devoir de faire, constamment, de mieux en mieux.

Nos modèles, par la beauté de leurs lignes, l'agrément de leur conduite, leur confort, la sécurité et l'économie de leur utilisation la justifient plus encore que leurs aînés.

Leurs carrosseries, que ce soient celles de nos 16 CV. 6 cyl. ou celles de, la belle 25 CV huit cylindres, d'une ligne surbaissée impeccable, sont larges et spacieuses.

La gamme de nos modèles classiques se complète, naturellement, pour chacun d'eux, d'un modèle digne héritier de notre glorieux passé sportif:

vifs, gais, de belle allure et pleins d'entrain, "ce sont nos Types Sport"

Laissez-moi le bon espoir que vous accueillerez les uns et les autres avec autant de plaisir que nous avons pris de soin à les concevoir et à les réaliser.

L. Delâge.

*A sales piece by Louis Delage describing his "Lovely, fun, fast, and full of spirit" beautiful French car.*

d'élégance of the 1930s. This model was produced in several chassis sizes, normal, long, and sport, with a variety of options available. The price began at 64,000 French francs for a bare 1930 Type D8 Sport chassis, to which an additional 20,000 to 30,000 French francs could be added, depending on the coachbuilder selected. The Type D6, which had an equally high-quality chassis, met with similar approbation when it was offered for sale to the public in 1931. Thanks to its downsized and more affordable chassis, which was priced at 49,550 French francs with an additional 18,000 French francs for coachwork, the Type D6 was popular with coachbuilders and buyers alike, outselling the Type D8 model.

Throughout the development of both these models the company struggled with its finances, barely making ends meet. Competition with other car companies was cutthroat, and although these cars were sold to the powerful and very rich, sales inevitably were affected by the Great Depression of the 1930s. Louis Delage was obliged to sell assets and failed in his efforts to get his company back on sound financial footing. The Delage company as an independent entity was liquidated in 1935. After the complicated business transactions were complete and Delahaye had purchased the bulk of the Delage assets, Walter Watney, a French-British businessman who had been one of Louis Delage's major financial supporters since the company's troubles

M. LOUIS DELAGE

*Sales brochure produced by Delahaye for the Delage Type D6 showing different post-war styling options.*

began, bought the assets of the Delage race car division and made good on the company's debts. He then created S.N.A.D., a new Delage company that focused primarily on racing and special projects. A few years later, in 1938, Delahaye purchased additional Delage assets from S.N.A.D.

Despite the liquidation and acquisition, Delage had its own stand at the 1935 Paris Auto Salon that was separate from that of its purchaser, Delahaye, an arrangement that remained until 1938. A reduced but faithful team of Delage engineers studied the new range of 4- and 6-cylinder cars being produced by Delahaye, and were able to introduce some improvements. A resulting 8-cylinder model was offered at the 1936 Paris Auto Salon: the Type D8-120, a Delage creation built from Delahaye components. This car, which had Lockheed hydraulic-operated Bendix brakes, independent front-wheel suspension, and a 4-speed or Cotal semi-automatic transmission, quickly became the new flagship model, one of the marque's finest automobiles. It sold for 55,000 French francs for a bare chassis and 78,000 French francs for a complete car, and was chosen by the best coachbuilders and designers of the era for their custom-built bodies.

Of all the coachbuilders, Henri Chapron especially favored the Type D8-120, since its chassis was particularly suited to his conservative lines and allowed him to show off his sense of balance and masterful grasp of two-tone coloring. An article in the French magazine *La Vie Lyonnaise* discussed coachbuilders who used this model, stating "These are, let us not forget, 'Grand Luxe' bodies created by master coachbuilders of great renown," and concluding "This is how the Delage, queen of the road and concours d'élégance, retains its envied title: 'Delage... the beautiful French car.'"

With no break in production, Delahaye continued to roll out models under Delage's blue oval until 1939. Cars were made with Delahaye components but kept the Delage styling. During its first year, the newly joined companies sold approximately 1000 Delage and 1200 Delahaye models; 30 percent less than expected, but reasonable considering economic problems and worker strikes.

Production by Delahaye of Delage chassis continued after the war until 1953, when Delahaye finally closed its doors. From the liquidation and subsequent rebirth in 1935 until World War II, the name Louis Delage afforded prestige to the revived brand, which was always marketed as having the company's founder at its head. After 1945, however, his direct involvement diminished. Louis Delage died in 1947 and was buried in the Le Pecq cemetery.

*On the Montlhéry racetrack on February 16, 1947. From left to right - drivers Louis Gérard, Maurice Varet, and Fernand Blanchi, all racing Delage Type D6-Ss.*

LE DE FRANCE
9778-RP2

# 1918 DELAGE BK

## *CHASSIS 6344*

## *COACHBUILDER: UNKNOWN*

The Type BK was created in late 1915 and was built, at a cost of 14,000 French francs, for the French Army to transport officers in World War I. Its motor was a straight six-cylinder model with a displacement of 2.66-liters. The head had fixed side valves, the carburetor was a Claudel NZ or Zenith D 30, the ignition was a Bosch Magneto, and the transmission was a 4-speed manual. The car's suspension was of a conventional spring design, similar to that of the touring Type AK, but the Type BK's springs were placed under its axle, which reduced ground clearance. Wire wheels were originally utilized, but when superior steel wheels appeared on the market, they were installed for the extra strength they provided on the muddy roads of a battlefield. Very few of these cars were built during World War I, and only a handful of Type BKs survive today. Open, lightweight coachwork was generally employed for this model, although documents from the period also show landaulet bodies with twin rear wheels.

While the coachbuilder of Chassis 6344 is unknown, it is likely one of the cars completed by the Delage factory for military purposes. This car is in very good original condition, having been in storage for more than fifty years as part of the Schlumpf Reserve Collection. Chassis 6344 is now part of the Mullin Collection.

*Top: An early-style Delage chassis plate. Although many such plates were made, only a handful survived World War I.*

*Middle: The car has two hand brakes.*

*Bottom: The door panels have custom pockets with initials.*

DELAGE

| Type BK | |
|---|---|
| Désignation du type | **BK (6 séries)** |
| Présentation aux Mines | 23/12/1915 |
| Prototype n° | **5690 moteur # 623** |
| **MOTEUR**<br>Type | DELAGE 6 K<br>6 cylindres en ligne monobloc. collecteur d'échappement rapporté sur cylindre. |
| Cylindrée ; alésage ; course | 2 662 cm$^3$ ; 66 x 130 |
| Puiss. administrative / réelle. | 13 CV / 27 ch |
| Distribution | Soupapes latérales. Distribution par chaînes. |
| Culasse | Moteur borgne. |
| Lubrification | Sous pression par pompe à engrenages et barbotage (vilebrequin perforé). Niveau 3 à 5 litres. Manomètre de pression d'huile sur le tablier. Clapet de surpression. |
| Alimentation | Carburateur Claudel NZ 20 ou Zénith D 30 (Série 6)<br>Réservoir d'essence sous l'auvent. (40 litres) |
| Allumage | Magnéto Bosch ZF 6 ou S.L.B B6 ou Gibaud B6 |
| Refroidissement | Circulation d'eau par pompe centrifuge.Ventilateur à courroie |
| EMBRAYAGE | À cône cuir et ressorts de progressivité. |
| BOÎTE / PONT<br>Nombre rapports<br>Type pont | Transmission par arbre à double cardan.<br>Boîte mécanique. 4 vitesses et marche AR par double baladeur.<br>4$^e$ en prise directe. Pignons à taille droite. Couple conique à taille droite puis spirale.<br>Démultiplications possibles : 15 x 61 ; 15 x 58 ; 15 x 55 |
| CHÂSSIS | Éléments en acier embouti rivetés.<br>**Suspensions** : ressorts à lames droites, semi-elliptiques<br>Montés sous le pont pour surbaissement du véhicule.<br>(AV : 900 x 55, AR : 1 300 x 55) |
| DIRECTION | Boîtier à vis et secteur. Avec manette des gaz sur le volant. |
| FREINS | 2 freins sur tambours arrière (par pédale), 1 sur la boîte de vitesses (par levier).<br>Commande par tiges rigides et palonnier.<br>Poulies de freins venues de fonderie avec les moyeux<br>Diam. des poulies AR : 350 mm Diam. du tambour : 220 mm |
| ROUES | Rayons bois de 820 x 120 ou Rudge à la demande.<br>(920 x 120 sur châssis coloniaux) |
| DIMENSIONS GÉNÉRALES<br>Voie, empattement (en m)<br>Autres données : poids du châssis, performances, etc. | Vitesse max. : environ 75 km/h<br>1,40 m x 3,36 m<br>Poids en ordre de marche 900 kg environ. |
| RENSEIGNEMENTS COMPLÉMENTAIRES | Le type BK est formé à partir du type AK surbaissé et légèrement modifié.<br>Consommation env. 15,5 l / 100 km<br>Tout appareillage électrique Bosch |

*Specifications for the Delage Type BK.*

*A Delage Type BK with a standard factory body. Note the steel wheels, which provided extra strength for driving on the muddy roads and battlefields of World War I.*

# 1923 DELAGE DE

*CHASSIS 12040*

*COACHBUILDER: M. TAUBES*

It was in 1922 that the factory produced Chassis 12040, a Delage Type DE. The model was first introduced at the 1921 Paris Auto Salon, and it entered production the following year. In 1919, after World War I, Louis Delage had made the erroneous decision to produce only "high-class" cars. In doing so, he seriously misjudged the public of post-war France, who were financially exhausted. The Type DE, however, sold well and returned Delage to its place as an automotive competitor. So well-conceived and built was this model from its very beginning that it neither evolved nor improved during its career—an almost unheard of achievement among cars! The Type DE had a 4-cylinder, 2.17-liter in-line engine with five main bearings, one Zenith carburetor, eight overhead valves, and a 3.18 m wheelbase. It was powerful for a small car, capable of a top speed of 103 kph. It also had four-wheel brakes, an uncommon feature at that time, which were capable of stopping the car within 100 meters. Total production of this model was 3600 cars.

The coachwork of Chassis 12040 was built by Taubes in Paris, a small firm that specialized in Delage and other luxury brands in the 1920s. The body is very similar to that of Bequet's record-breaking car from the 1922 Paris to Madrid run. However, this particular Delage has several features typical of a Grand Tourer: a horizontally split windshield, a collapsible windscreen for the rear seat, twin side-mounted spare tires, rear jump seats, a spotlight, and a rear luggage rack. The car remained in Europe until 2005, when it was imported to the United States and given a sympathetic restoration. In 2006, Peter Mullin purchased Chassis 12040, and it remains, well preserved, in the Mullin Collection.

La Carrosserie Universelle
M. Taubes
27, Rue St Sabin - PARIS - Tel. Roq. 43.

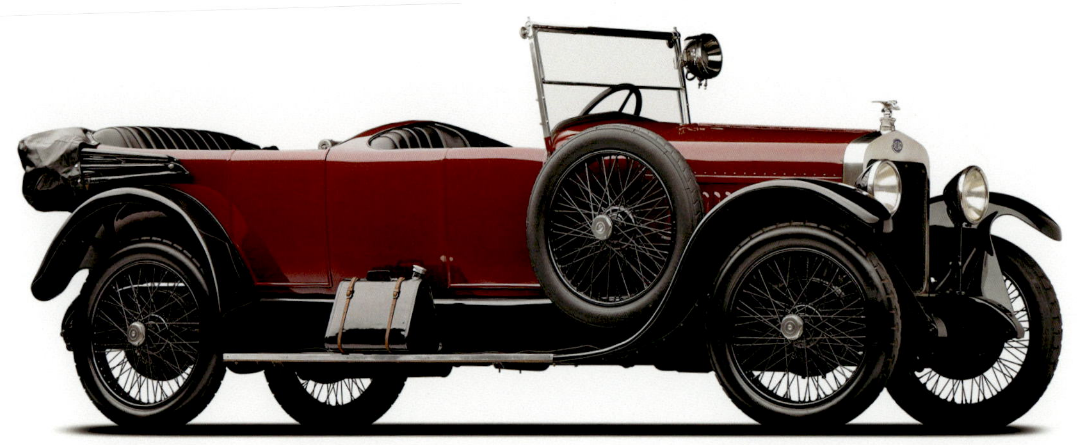

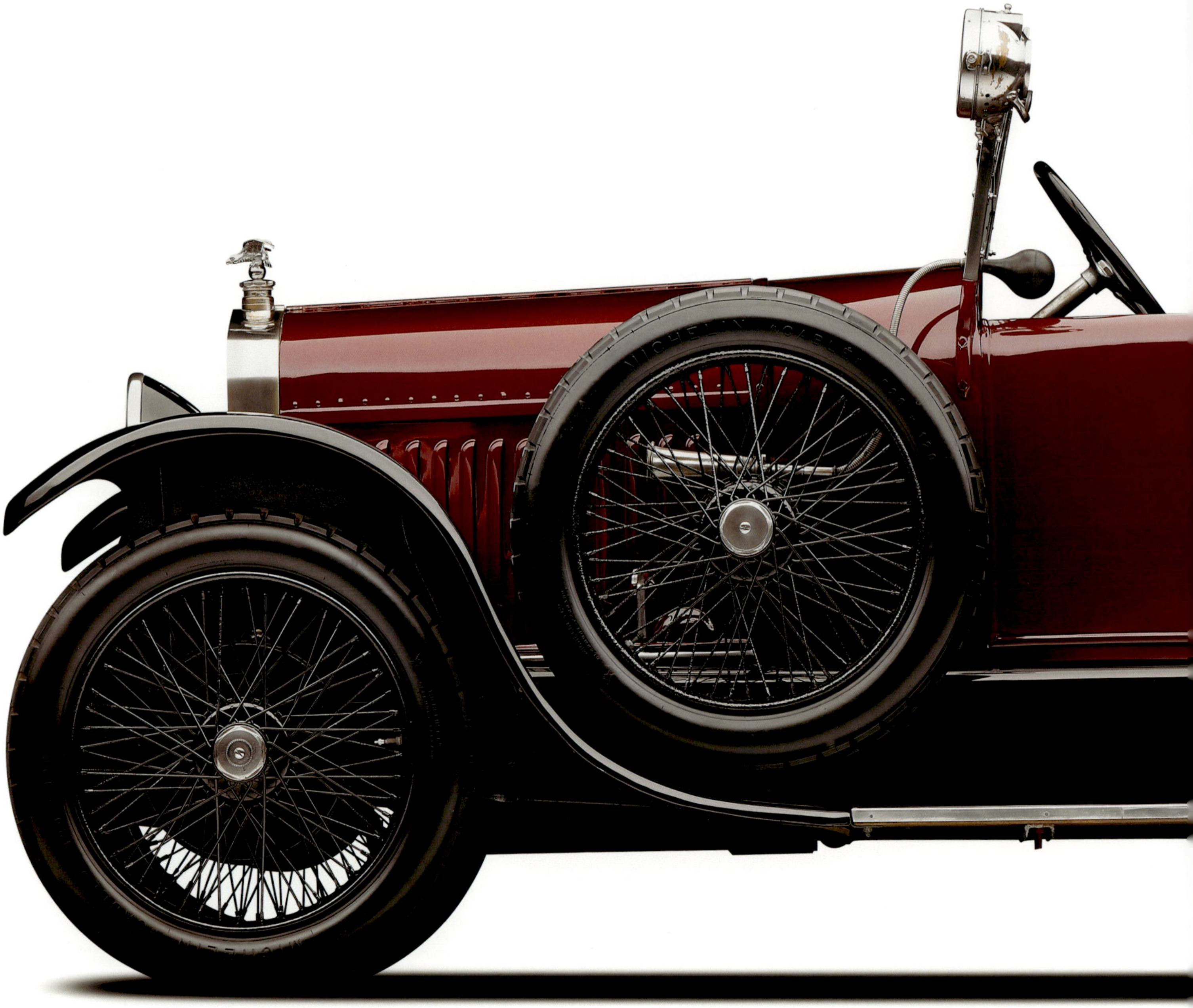

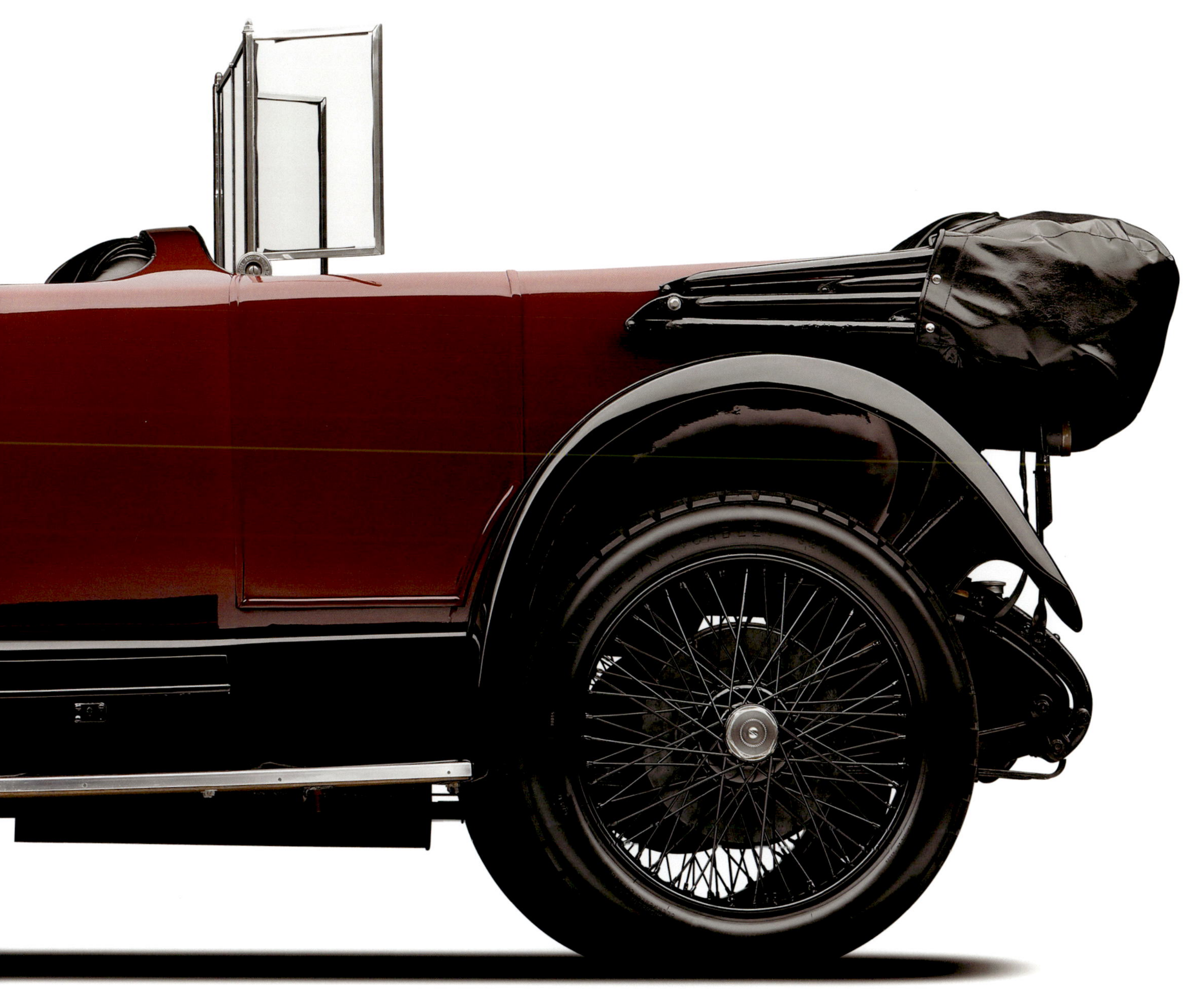

*The Delage Type DE was usually chauffeur driven during its era of popularity. This was standard form when going for a Sunday drive or to a concours d'élégance.*

*Facing page, top: Delage 4-cylinder engine with downdraft carburetor.*
*Facing page, bottom: The repetition of curved shapes is a very French style.*

# 1927/1936 DELAGE ERA

*CHASSIS 6*

*COACHBUILDER: DELAGE FACTORY*

The Delage ERA in the Mullin Collection, identified as Chassis 6, is a Type 15-S-8. It emerged from the factory in 1927 as a blue grand prix model, and it brought the Delage company the title of World Construction Champion. In 1936, almost a decade later, British championship driver Dick Seaman was still winning races with this grand prix car.

Prince Chula Chakrabongse of Siam (modern day Thailand) purchased the grand prix for his cousin, Prince Bira, to drive. Uneasy about Bira's royal welfare inside a ten-year-old chassis, Prince Chula asked his mechanic, Giulio Ramponi, to update the car. Ramponi contacted the Delage factory, which commissioned Albert Lory to design a new chassis featuring the latest technology in independent front-wheel suspension; Lory had created the original car ten years previously, and he still worked for the new Delage company, S.N.A.D. The new chassis, Chassis 5, was fabricated by Rubery Owen in England; it had a Delage straight-eight engine similar to that of the original 1927 grand prix.

Unfortunately, the new chassis was stiffer and heavier than the original, which probably accounted for Prince Bira's lack of success with the car, and although he drove it occasionally, he never raced it seriously. With the onset of World War II in 1939, the Delage was sold to English race car driver Reg Parnell, who also bought Chassis 6, a spare chassis that Owen had built. Parnell completed Chassis 6 in 1946, giving it a body and a Delage straight-eight engine like that of its brother.

Rob Walker, famous driver and owner of the Rob Walker Racing Team, purchased Chassis 6 in 1949 for competition purposes. In 1950, he commissioned Freddie Dixon to get the car in running condition. Unfortunately, Dixon replaced the car's blower with a Wade supercharger, and the result was irreparable damage to every Delage engine used in the car. When Walker realized that his supply of such engines had been exhausted, he chose to find an alternative with a bit more power: "After that first season with the Delage we had no engines left, so when Peter Walker's E-Type ERA came up for sale, we bought it. It had been going well, and we thought at the time it had the most potent 1-1/2-liter engine available." Following that logic, Walker purchased and installed the two-stage supercharged E-Type ERA engine, which he later claimed was the most difficult engine he ever worked with. It was at this juncture that the Delage ERA was born.

Walker campaigned the car successfully for three years before selling it in 1954. It passed to Alan Burnard, who drove it for a short time before selling it again, at which point it went through a varied succession of owners: Jack Goodhew, Ian Kerr, R.W. Potter, Patrick Lindsay, Anthony Mayman, and Bruce Spollon. During the mid-1970s, it was raced successfully in vintage competitions. Peter Mullin finally acquired the car in 2006.

*Facing page: Prince Bira of Siam, sitting atop his Delage, toasts the crowd after winning the International Trophy Race at the Brooklands racetrack on February 5, 1936.*

*Following pages: The Delage ERA sans engine, as an engine rebuild was being performed at time of photography.*

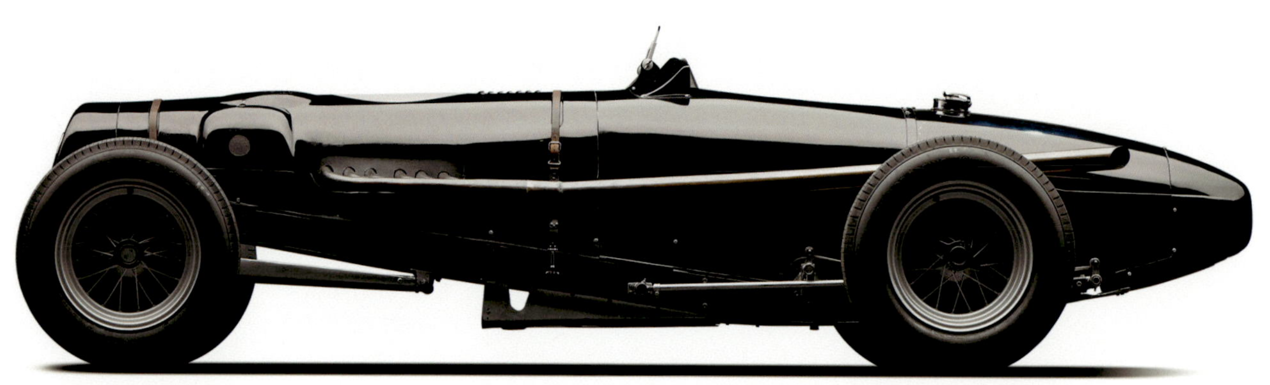

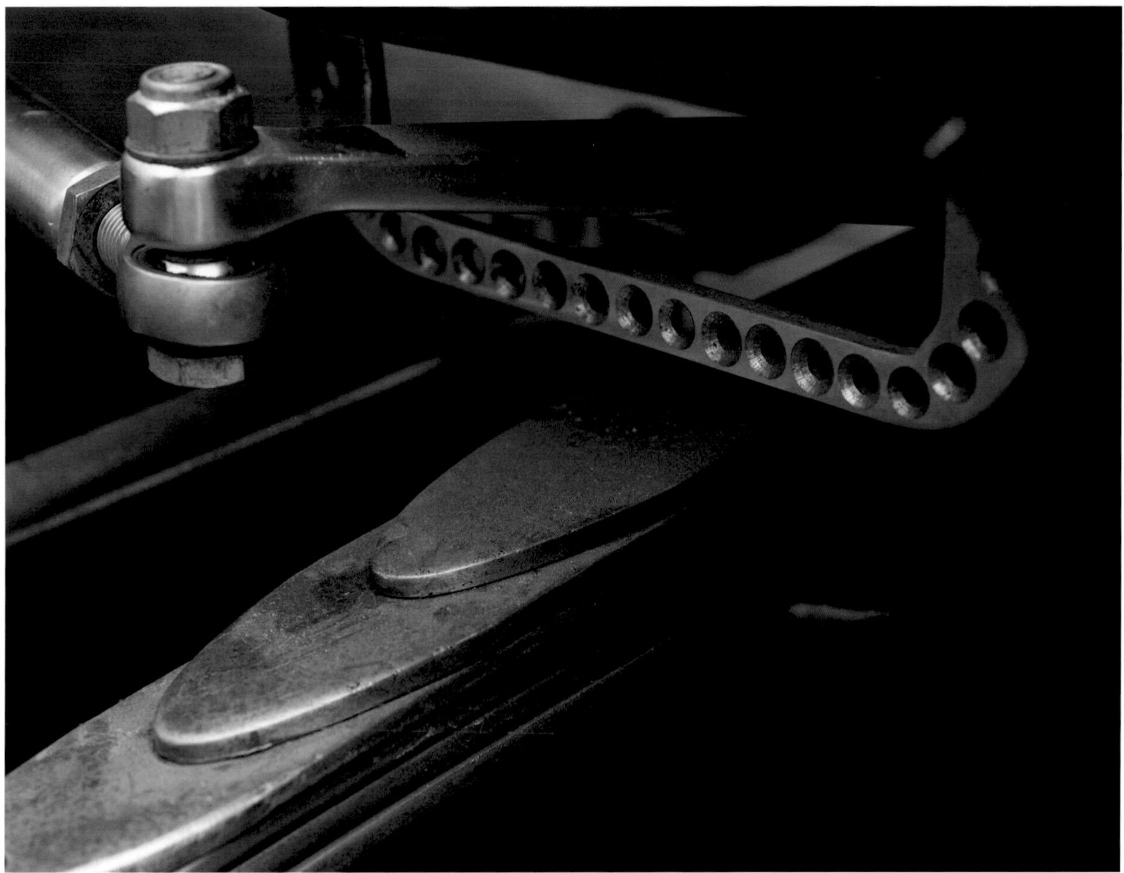

*Top and bottom: Elegant components of the Delage ERA suspension and steering linkage.*
*Facing page: In November 1940, the car was owned by Reg Parnell and had a Delage straight-eight engine.*

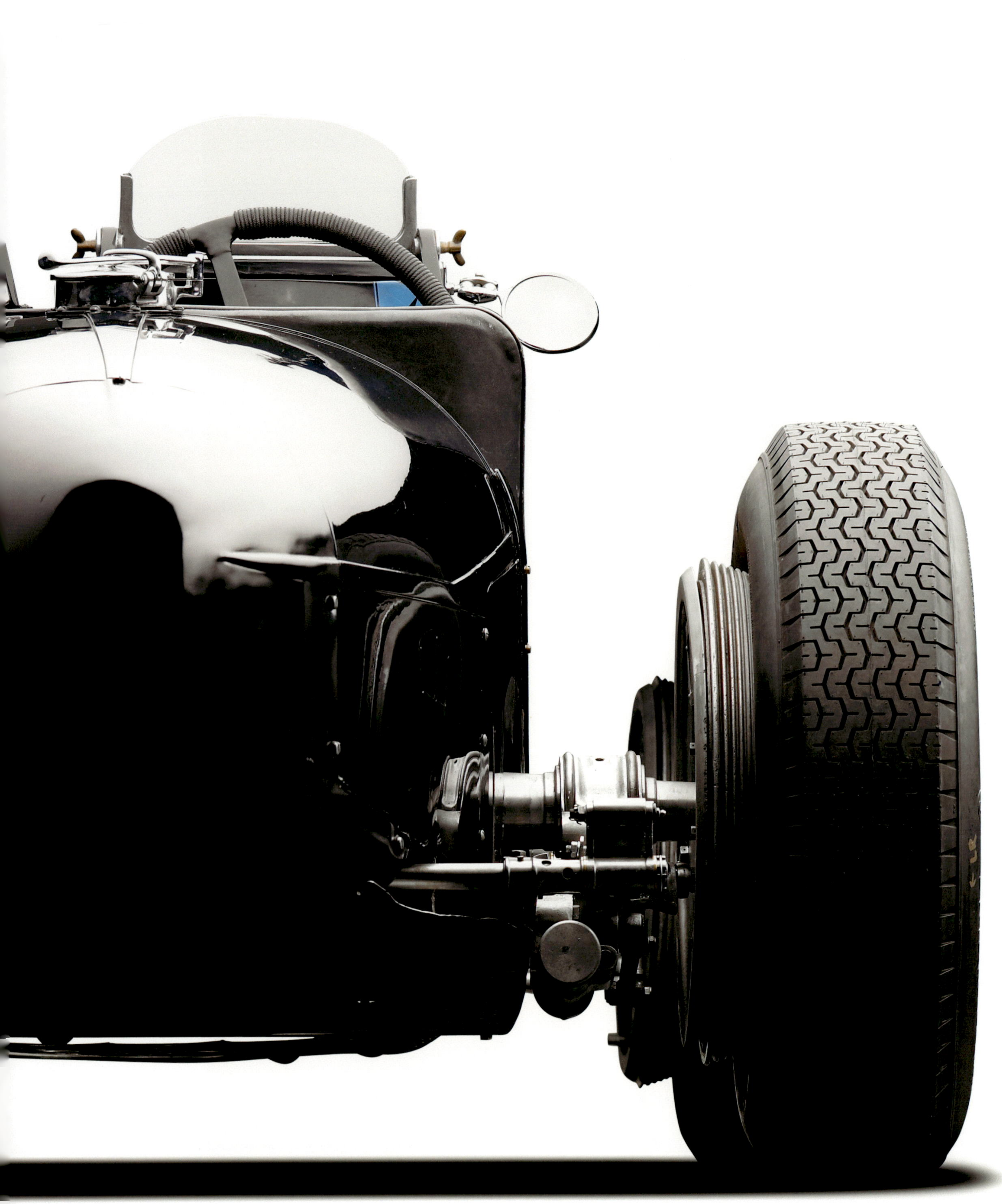

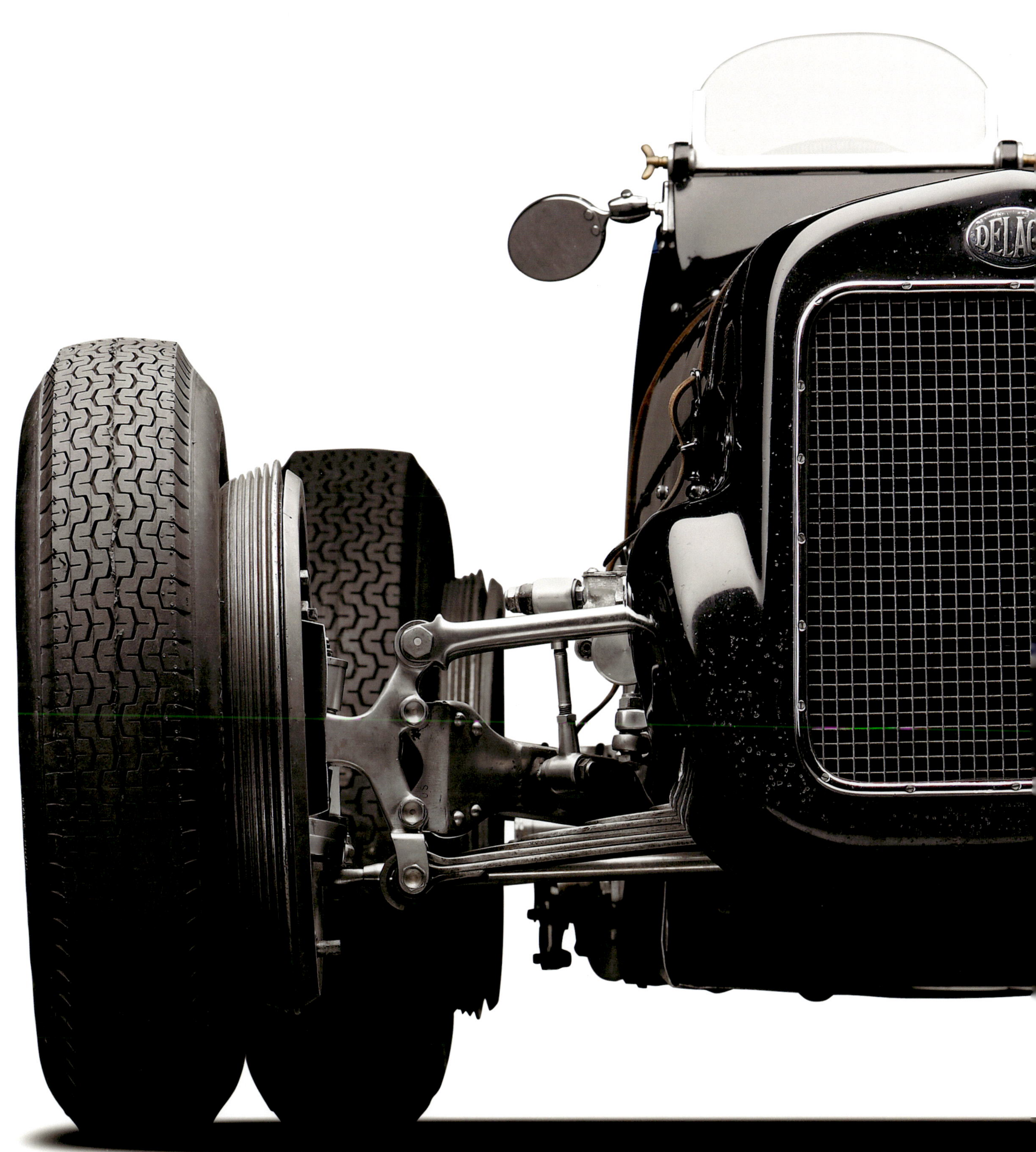

# 1932 DELAGE D8-S

## *CHASSIS 36025*

## *COACHBUILDER: DUVIVIER*

The Type D8-S in the Mullin Collection is an upgraded model that came out in 1931. Delage expert and author Daniel Cabart explains the differences:

> *Checking the D8-S factory list confirms that the numbers match, and engine number 26-S corresponds to the car number for this chassis. The S engine features some very special devices, such as heating of the carburetor manifold by oil circulation (instead of water coming from the head, through the manifold and then to the radiator), cooling the oil via pipes in the sump, and a very special rocker arrangement (first fitted on aircraft engines) similar to the D6-11 and D8-15 system. The jet sizes and arrangements are also different, as is the camshaft and timing.*

The Delage Type D8 was first introduced in 1929 with a straight-eight, 4.06-liter engine that could develop 108 bhp at 2500 rpm. The car was powerful, the engine quiet, and the handling good, so much so that the British journalists quickly dubbed it "The French Rolls-Royce." The Type D8 also had great potential for further development, which British importers took advantage of by producing an upgraded version called the Type D8 Super Sport 100. It was guaranteed to reach a speed of 100 mph and was quite successful in Britain and the United States.

Delage abandoned the grand prix circuit after 1927 but still wanted to be recognized as the World Champion marque. Confident in the qualities of this car, the company prepared a standard Type D8-S model with track bodywork. The result competed at Montlhéry, where it broke ten international records in 1931 and nine more in 1932, proving that Delage could still produce world-class cars.

The Type D8-S had cable brakes that worked well, and thanks to its 20 mpg the car became an instant favorite with the motoring elite. The chassis was relatively low slung for a full-sized car and its elongated engine compartment allowed for a long hood that balanced the car's proportions. *La Vie Automobile* of November 25, 1929, said: "French engineering, when it is inspired by the lessons of the racetrack, has no need of huge, gas-guzzling engines to achieve most remarkable performances with unusually vigorous responses."

Chassis 36025 was bodied by Duvivier, a small luxury coachbuilder on the outskirts of Paris, well known for high-quality coachwork on the leading marques. It was in business from 1919 to 1932, at which time it merged with Gallé, another Paris luxury coachbuilder with the motto "Only the line itself creates Elégance." The coachwork on this Delage was one of the last produced by Duvivier as an independent entity. The car was shown by Madame Ira Morris at the 1932 Paris Concours d'Élégance, where it took the category for two-door all-weather models.

After the concours, ownership of this car is a mystery until after World War II, when it was acquired by the Schlumpf brothers. It was put in their reserve collection at Malmerspach to wait its turn for restoration, and remained there for fifty years while a legal dispute raged on concerning ownership. It was then purchased in 2009 with the rest of the reserve collection by Peter Mullin. The car is in completely original condition, exactly as it was when put away many years ago.

*Facing page; This Delage D8-S was owned by Madame Ira Morris. It is pictured at the L'Auto Concours d' 'Élégance on June 19, 1932, where it placed first in the category for all-weather two-door coachwork.*

*The distributor advance is on the steering wheel. The dashboard is beautiful and well preserved.*

*The doors were made with pockets for personal items.*

# 1939 DELAGE D8-120

## *CHASSIS 51760*
## *COACHBUILDER:* Henri Chapron

The Delage D8-120, Chassis 51760, (body number 6089), and was delivered by Henri Chapron on June 21, 1939. It was from the second series of the model, and as such had a lower and lighter chassis than its predecessor. The engine of the Type D8-120 had aluminum pistons with four rings, steel connecting rods, and overhead valves. The car possessed a single two-barrel downdraft carburetor and a Cotal electric planetary transmission. Chassis 51760 was designed by Chapron as a four-place cabriolet with a three-position top. The instruments on the dashboard are exceptionally well balanced and surrounded by wood trim. The rear of the car is in the "bustle back" style, with a covered spare tire and top-loading trunk.

Its early history was colorful, as it was reportedly appropriated by a French general of the Vichy government who was a German collaborator. In 1946, after the war's end, the general sent the car to California but was unable to obtain a visa for himself, so he went to Argentina and sold the car to RKO Studios.

In Hollywood, the car's graceful and conservative styling earned it a role in the 1951 classic *An American in Paris*. For the film, the producers commissioned certain changes to the car's design, including taillight modifications and a new green paint job. Chapron himself was involved in the alterations. The film showed Gene Kelly being chauffeured around the City of Lights in the Delage with actress Nina Foch.

When the movie was completed, the car was returned to Los Angeles, where it was acquired in 1955 by Thol "Si" Simonson, a member of the RKO Studios production team. He took the car in lieu of the $15,000 in severance pay he was owed by RKO. Si drove the Delage around California before putting it up for auction in 1987, at which time Peter Mullin bought the car after consulting with Jim Hull. Mr. Mullin has displayed Chassis 51760 at major concours d'élégance ever since with great results; the car, with its beautiful proportions and elegant Chapron touch, is a wonderful example of French automotive elegance.

DELAGE

1052 G 75

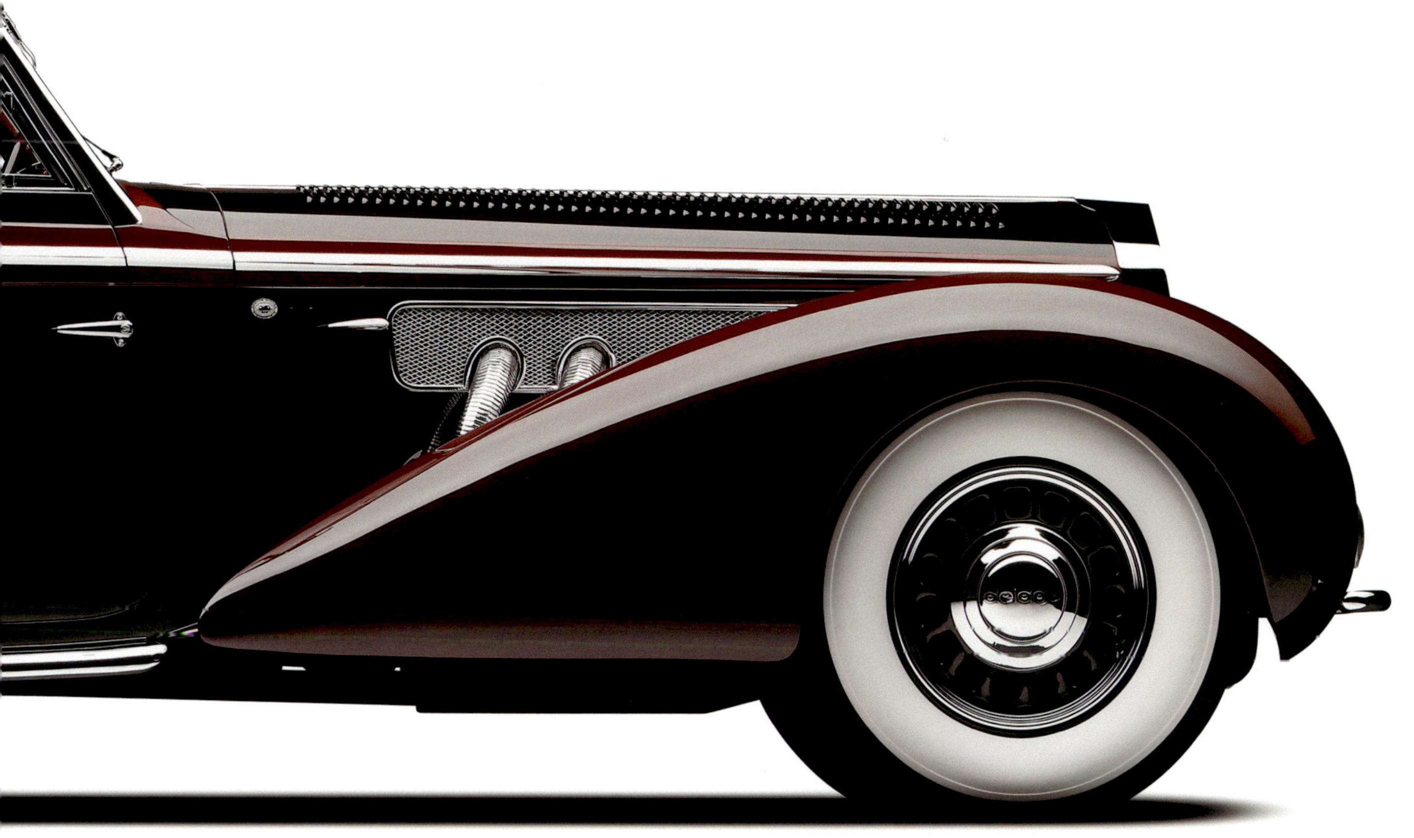

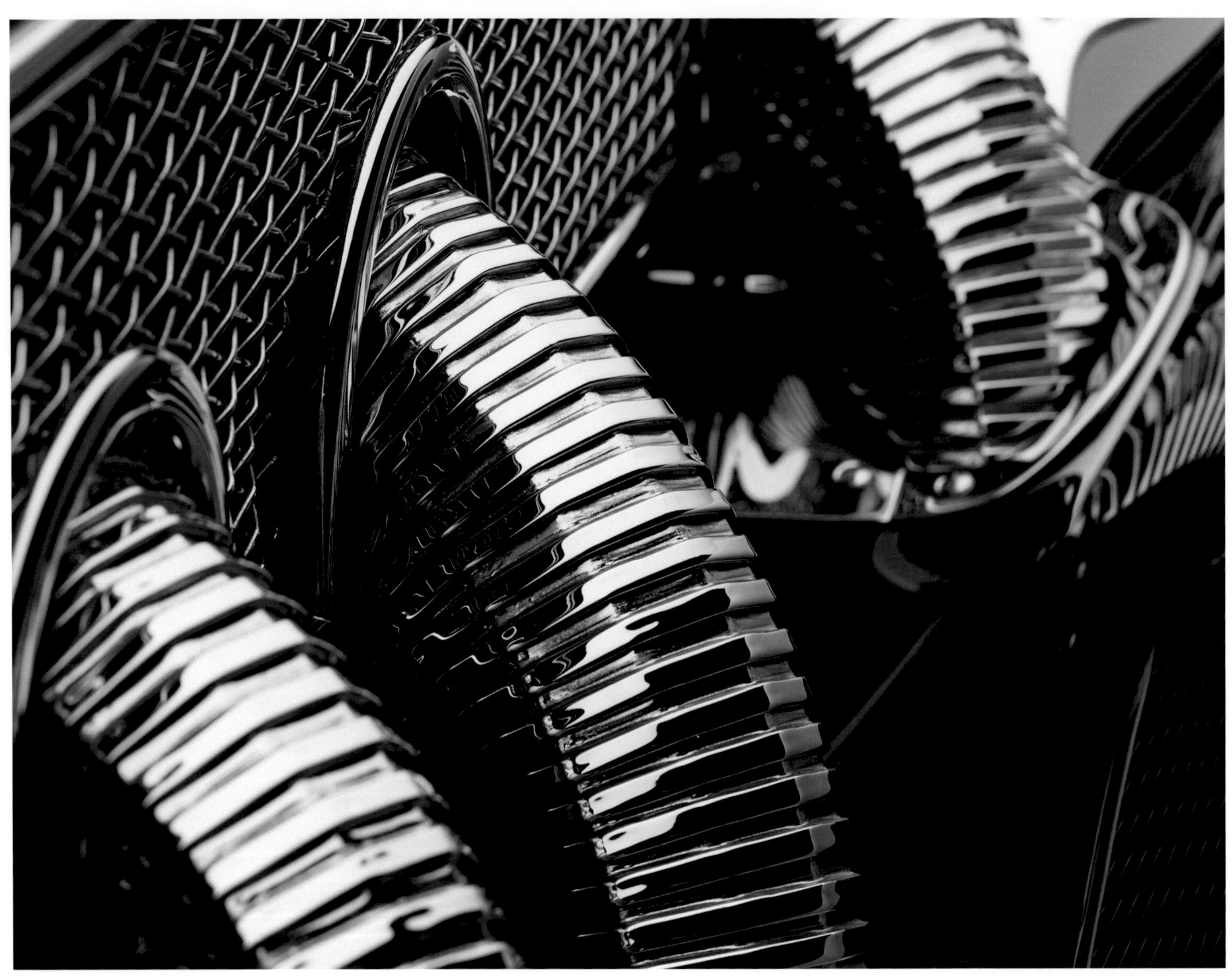

*The exhaust pipes are sleeved with flexible chrome pipe to moderate the heat. These sleeves are also a decorative, sculptural element.*

*The valve cover is engine turned.*

# 1946 DELAGE D6-3L

*CHASSIS 880004*

*COACHBUILDER: UNKNOWN*

When World War II started in September 1939, competitive racing was suspended during the German occupation of France. But almost as soon as the conflict ended, the French returned to their love affair with racing. In 1946, the Société Anonyme de Fabrication des Automobiles Delage (SAFAD, previously S.N.A.D., see page 137), which was under the management of owner Walter Watney, built five Type D6-3L race cars for the 1947 season. The vehicles had open two-seat bodies and were successfully raced throughout Europe for the next three years. The horsepower of the post-war Type D6-3Ls had been improved to 142 bhp at 5300 rpm; each weighed 950 kg and had a maximum speed of just over 210 kph.

Of the five Type D6-3L race cars, Chassis 880004 was campaigned the most frequently. It was purchased in 1947 by race car driver Henri Louveau, who frequently entered it in competitive events. Louveau drove the car to a second place finish at the 1947 Grand Prix of Perpignan and a third place finish at the Grand Prix of Marseilles that same year. The car also took sixth at the 1947 Grand Prix of Italy, this time with Maurice Varet behind the wheel. In 1948, Chassis 880004 came in fifth at the Grand Prix des Nations and second at the Grand Prix des Frontiers. The following year, Louveau drove the car at both Le Mans and the Grand Prix of Spa-Francorchamps, finishing second in both races.

Louveau entered the car at Le Mans again in 1950, this time finishing in seventh place. A short time later, the car was put up for sale and eventually purchased by Jacques Nollé in 1953. In 1955, Nollé had Chassis 880004 rebodied as a coupé by coachbuilder Pichon & Parat. But afterward, Nollé had difficulty registering the car for racing, so he sold it to Richard Gallagher, an American serviceman stationed in France. Gallagher later sold the Type D6-3L to another American soldier, who eventually went home to the United States and took the car with him. It stayed on the East Coast for many years until 2002, when Peter Mullin purchased it and had it restored to its original 1947 racing configuration by Ateliers de Touraine.

*Facing page: The 12 Hours of Paris at Montlhéry on September 12, 1948; Henri Louveau and Robert Brunet drove Chassis 880004 to a second place finish.*

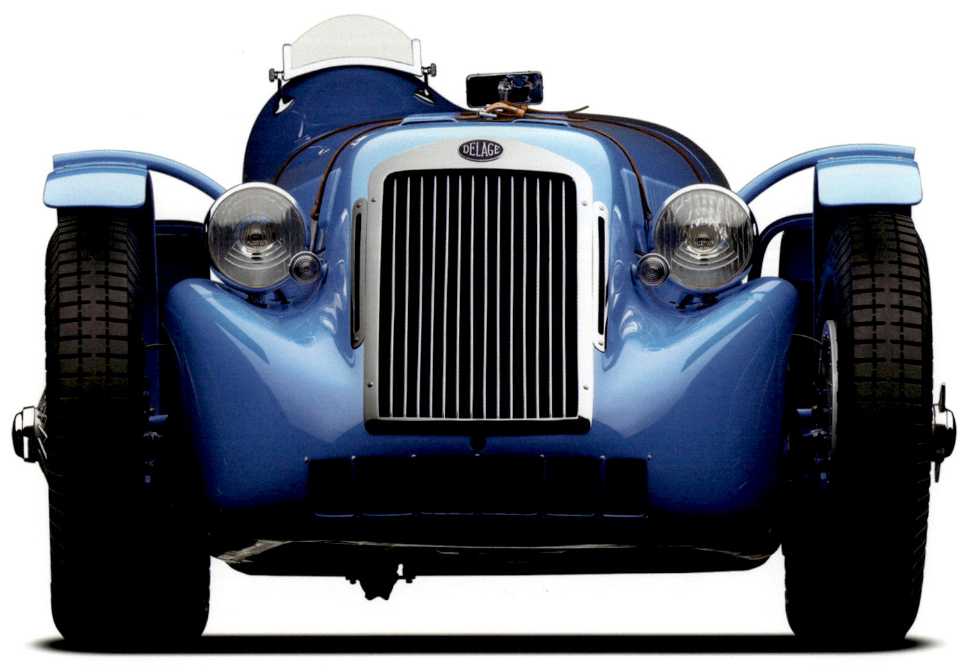

ECURIE
FRANCE
ENGLEBERT

Nº
TOURS FAITS
12
200
DELAGE
14
1

*Henri Louveau and Juan Jover drive the Delage Type D6-3l to a first in class and second overall finish at Le Mans on June 25 and 26, 1949. They were beaten by Ferrari's first Le Mans entry, a Type 166 driven by Luigi Chinetti and Lord Selsdon.*

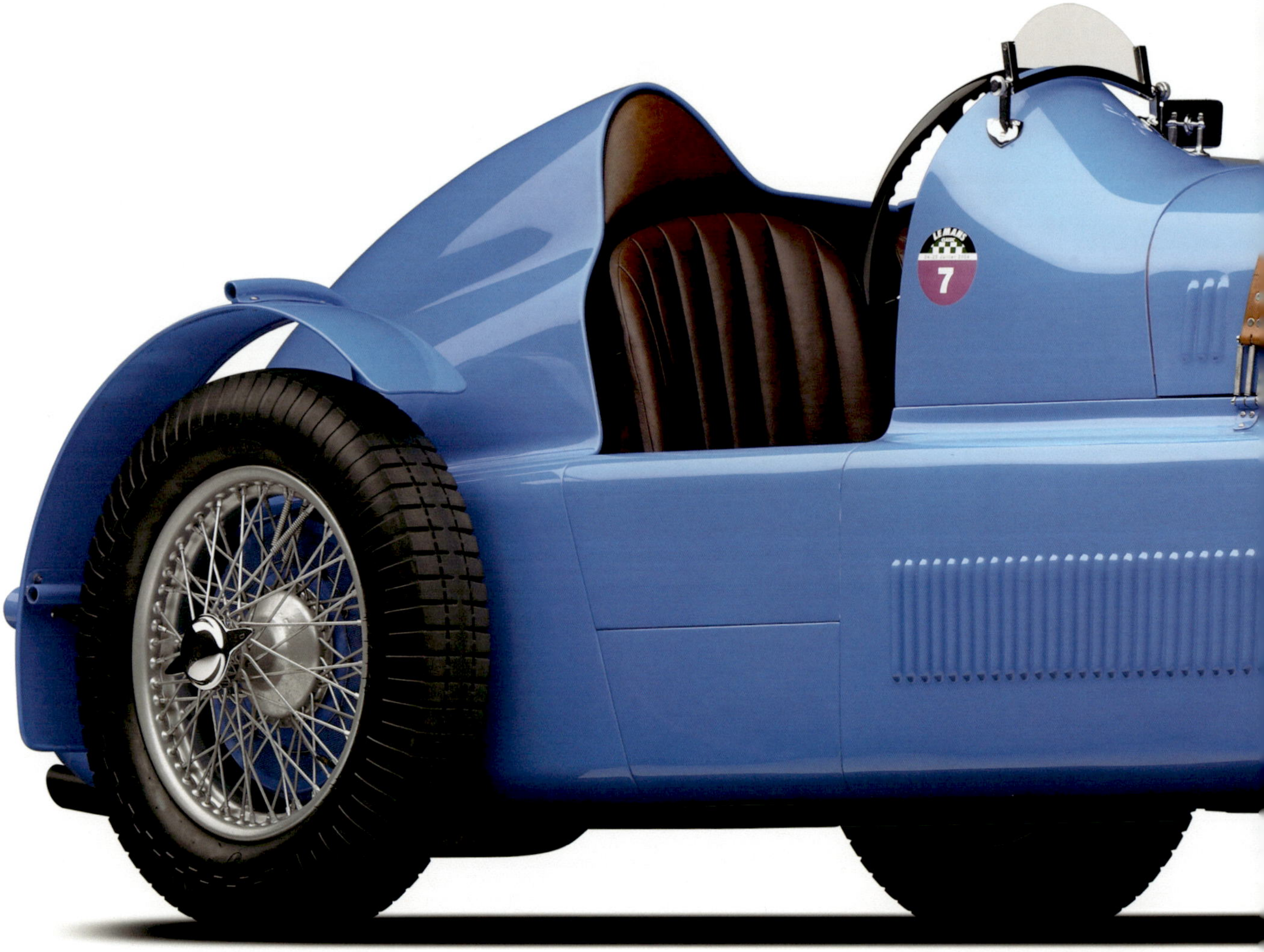

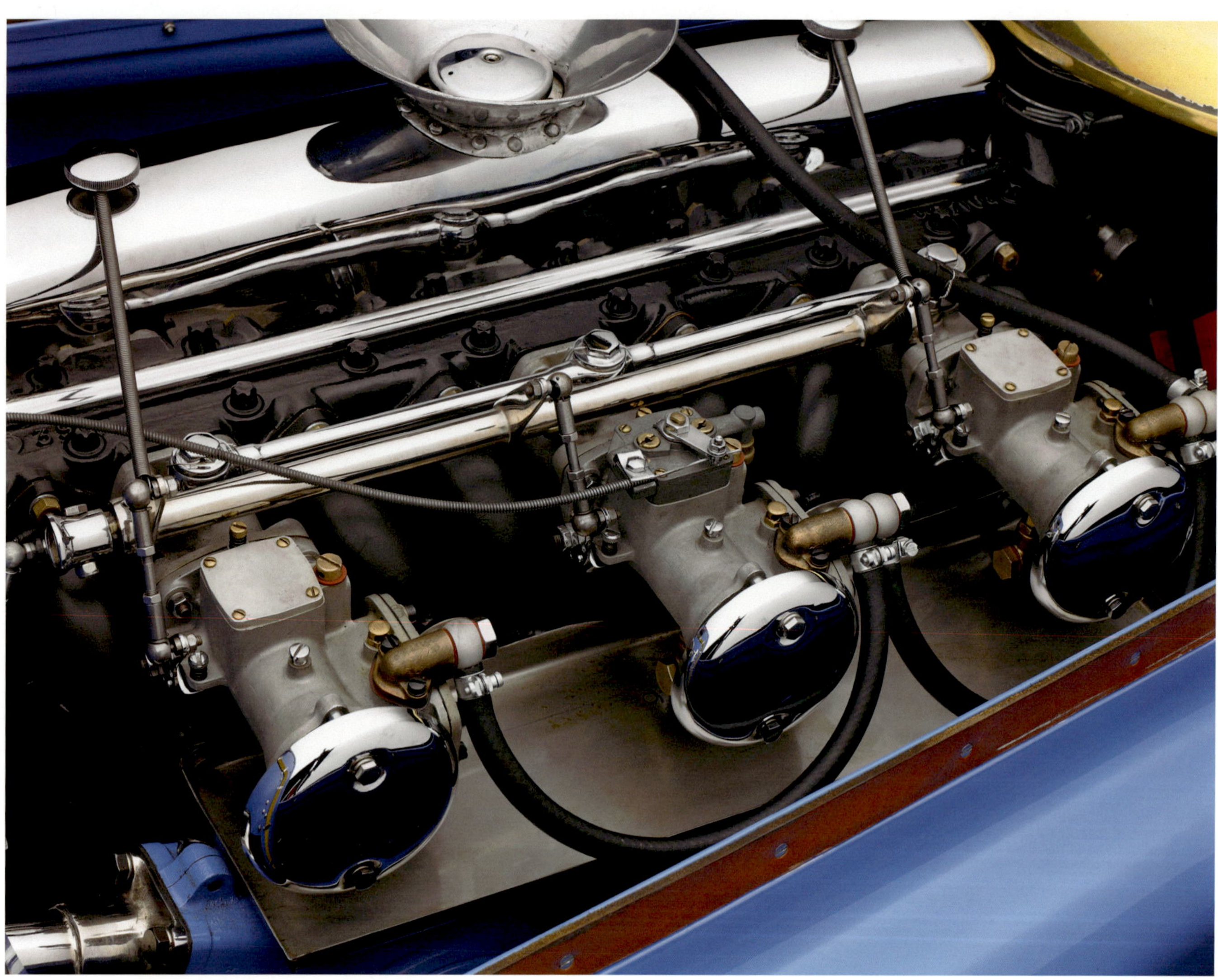

*The three Solex carburetors.*

*Quick release racing gas cap.*

TALBO
SURESNES

# TALBOT-LAGO

13
13

# A BRIEF HISTORY OF TALBOT-LAGO

The origins of the Talbot-Lago company can be traced to Sunbeam-Talbot-Darracq (S.T.D.), an Anglo-French conglomerate with a complicated corporate structure and unreliable profits. This company sold Sunbeam and Talbot cars in England (where they were known as Tall-butts) and Darracq and Talbot cars in France (where they were known as Tahl-bows).

Antony "Tony" Lago, who worked for S.T.D., was an Italian with a long career in cars. Lago was born in Venice in 1893 and studied engineering at the Polytechnic School in Milan. He joined the Italian army during World War I, ending his military service in 1918 with the rank of major. In the early 1920s he went to England, working successively for Isotta-Fraschini, L.A.P. Engineering, and as a director of Wilson Self-Changing Gear, Ltd. It was in this last position that he helped develop the Wilson gear box he would later use in Talbot-Lago cars. In 1933, he joined S.T.D. as sub-director for Sunbeam at Wolverhampton, England.

At the time, S.T.D.'s French subsidiary had fallen into financial disarray, and the managers in England wanted to liquidate it. However, Lago persuaded the board to send him to the French factory to work on a new production focus. By 1934, he was appointed general director of Automobiles Talbot in Suresnes, France.

The next year, the English portion of the company was unexpectedly bought by the Rootes Group, and at the age of 42, Lago bought the Talbot-Darracq subsidiary in France, becoming its sole owner. He obtained a subsidy from the French government, enabling the company to stay afloat, and began to design cars under the Talbot-Lago marque.

It was Tony Lago's philosophy to equip production models with high-performance engines and dramatic coachwork and then showcase his cars on the racing circuit. He would take a detuned racing engine and install it in a car that was only slightly different from the racing version; the result would then be available for purchase by anyone rich enough to pay his price.

*Facing page: René Hanriot drives a 1906 Darracq V-8 at the Circuit des Ardennes in the Netherlands. This early motor developed 128 hp, making it one of the most powerful engines of its day.*

At the same time, he and his engineer, Walter Becchia, designed a powerful racing chassis that would also be used for touring cars. Lago became the only car manufacturer who could boast that his touring cars included genuine racing engines and chassis. Within a year of taking over the company, he came to the Paris Auto Salon with two new models, the Type 120 and the Type 150, both of which sparked great interest among car lovers.

Intent on racing, Lago wooed driver René Dreyfus away from the Scuderia Ferrari team and persuaded him to work as driver and manager of the new Talbot-Lago racing team. It took a while to work out the mechanical weak spots, but the Type 150-C immediately proved to be fast. Shape was a factor in the car's speed. Lago had consulted Jean Andreau, the engineering expert on aerodynamics, on the best design for the coachwork of the Talbot-Lago racing models. The Andreau design would also be used later for the coachwork of Lago's touring cars.

At their first race, the 1936 French Grand Prix, the Type 150-C Talbot-Lagos came in eigth, ninth, and tenth. At the French Grand Prix in 1937 they did much better, placing first, second, third, and fifth, beating the Delahayes and the Bugatti. Then, at the British Tourist Trophy at Donington Park that same year, drivers Gianfranco Comotti and René Le Bègue came in first and second, beating two Frazer-Nash models, two Singers, one Delahaye, and two Rileys. Grand prix racing, in which the Talbot-Lagos participated, was a hugely popular competitive sport throughout Europe. Manufacturers promoted their products by fielding their own factory teams, drivers became national heroes, and during those tense pre-World War II days, national pride was tied to outcomes on the track. It was Talbot-Lago's triumph at the 1937 French Grand Prix that brought international attention to the marque. The performance and extraordinary appearance of the new Type 150-C-SS created a sensation among the public. By this time, Tony Lago and Joseph Figoni started working together to produce the touring cars that would dominate the concours d'élégance from Paris to Nice in the late 1930s. These works of art catered to the demanding tastes and deep pockets of aristocrats and millionaires.

In 1936 Joseph Figoni created his gorgeous design for the Teardrop, the flowing curves of which, accented by brilliant colors, had never been seen before. A teardrop is the perfect aerodynamic shape for an object in motion, resembling the raindrops created by nature as they fall to earth. The entire look of the Talbot-Lago Teardrop epitomized speed, aerodynamic

*Facing page: Antony Lago (1893 – 1960) purchased the French Talbot Company in 1935 and reorganized it, basing his new cars on performance and styling.*

efficiency, and elegance. Of the fourteen Type 150-C-SS Teardrops produced by Figoni, thirteen still exist, a testimony to the love and care lavished upon them by their owners. Many survived World War II because they were bought by the Hollywood set and sent to the United States. The proud owners of these beauties have included French race car driver Marcel Balsa, Australian Olympic bobsledder Freddie McEvoy, Hollywood playboy Tommy Lee, and the Maharani of Khapurthala, who enjoyed changing her car's color scheme to match her latest outfit.

The French post-war economy was very hard on all French automobile manufacturers and coachbuilders, including Talbot-Lago. New regressive tax laws punished luxury cars manufactures with high taxes, specifically taxing those motors that displaced more than 2.5 liters. Raw materials were hard to get, and those clients who did have money were reluctant to spend it. The French clientele who had purchased extravagant cars before the war were, for the most part, uncomfortable with obvious displays of wealth during the years spent struggling to rebuild. As a result, companies like Delahaye, Delage, and Talbot-Lago increasingly targeted markets in the United States. The problem with the overseas market, however, was that its buyers wanted left-hand drive cars, and the French marques offered very few such models.

*The introduction of the Talbot-Lago T 150-C-SS at the National Automotive Show for 1938 models at New York City's Grand Central Palace on October 27, 1937. The model's styling was dubbed "New York" in honor of the event.*

*Figoni named this notch-backed model Jeancart after one of his big customers.*

Talbot-Lago resumed production in 1946 with the Type 26 Record, which had a new 4.5-liter, 6-cylinder motor that could develop 170 bhp; the car also had overhead valves and new hydraulic brakes. Tony Lago continued his pre-war strategy of basing his production cars on his race cars, a tactic that saved development money and allowed him to focus on racing, his real passion. The Talbot-Lago Grand Sport was born of this strategy, being based on the Type 26 Record and upgraded to more closely match the new Type 26-C Grand Prix race car, which was lighter and had a shorter chassis of 2.65 meters.

All of these models were introduced at the October 1947 Paris Auto Salon, the first salon after World War II. They were embraced by the leading coachbuilders of the day, several of who used the chassis to create stunning examples of their work; the Saoutchik Grand Sport, discussed later in this book, was one such example. However, the European economy was just beginning to pick up, and only 155 cars were sold that first year. The new Talbot-Lago Type 26 models were some of the highest priced cars marketed in 1947: at 1,340,000 French francs for a cabriolet and 1,851,000 French francs for a Grand Sport, they were more expensive than any model produced by Delahaye, Delage, or Ferrari.

For the 1948 Paris Auto Salon, Talbot-Lago kept to the Type 26 cabriolet and Grand Sport as its two basic models; to keep up cash flow, the company occasionally manufactured and sold pre-war Type 15s made from leftover parts. Marketing at the salon focused on the Grand Sport, as sports cars were very popular with the public, especially in the United States and United Kingdom, and sales increased to 233 cars. That year, Talbot-Lago also brought forth its first race car for the new Formula One rule: the single-seat Type 26-C.

Along with the Type 26 Record and Grand Sport, the 1949 Paris Auto Salon featured a new Type 15 L,

*This model, New York, was named after its successful showing in the 1937 National Automotive Show in New York City.*

nicknamed the Lago Baby. It was less expensive than the other post-war models, the prices of which were rising rapidly because of inflation. The Lago Baby could be had with a 4- or 6-cylinder motor, either of which displaced 2.7-liters. The car initially sparked clients' interest, and combined sales rose to a peak of 433 models. But this modest boost could not fix the company's financial situation, and by the end of 1950, Talbot-Lago was in deep trouble. The cost of developing the Type 15 L and the expense of maintaining a racing team had pressed the company to its limit. Tony Lago was not focused on his passenger cars, but rather on his sports and race cars, the latter of which had just won a major victory at Le Mans. He finally lost heart, energy, and courage—to keep the company out of his creditors' hands, he laid off workers and took out a loan to keep Talbot-Lago in business.

Sales were disastrous in 1951. The new Type 15 LB was underpowered, and the car's performance failed to stimulate much business, even with a price lower than those of the other models. Clients did not like the Type 26 Record's factory styling, and only eleven chassis were sold. The company's combined sales for that year was a mere eighty cars. The racing team was expensive and even with a few victories and podium finishes, it did not generate sales for the touring cars. The 1951 Paris Auto Salon featured refreshed versions of the Types 15 LB and 26, but the buying public had become disenchanted with such touring cars and preferred to focus on the Grand Sport, which was doing well in racing events. The following year's salon offered little that was new in the way styling or models, and only thirty-four cars were sold. With only a handful of Type 15 LBs sold, the company dropped the car from production in late 1953 to focus on the Grand Sport, which was updated that year. But the competition was the Jaguar XK-120, which cost less and caught more attention than the Grand Sport, which had been re-designated the GSL.

Talbot-Lago bodied the majority of the Type 26 chassis with the GSL coachwork, but sales were again limited, too much so to offset the high French taxes. At the 1955 Paris Auto Salon, the Type 26 Record was dropped and the Grand Sport was displayed for the last time. A new model was also offered, a coupé with a 2.5-liter, 4-cylinder motor and a factory body designed by Carlo Delaisse. These models were the last of the Talbot-Lago-powered cars to be built. From 1955 until the end of production, the company purchased engines from other manufacturers, as it could no longer afford to build its own. Several private individuals raced specials at Le Mans and other events, but with little success. The soul of Talbot-Lago was gone.

In 1959, a year before Tony Lago's death, his company was purchased by French automaker Simca. Talbot-Lago had produced only five thousand cars over a twenty-five-year period, but they were landmark models. Strother MacMinn states, "The Talbot Coupé represents what may be one of the finest examples of assembled form applied to the automobile." Chrysler later purchased the Simca brand, and Peugeot now owns the Talbot-Lago marque: it will be interesting to see what they do with it.

*Boxing champion Sugar Ray Robinson settles into a Talbot-Lago at the Grand Prix de Paris in 1951.*

# 1929 SUNBEAM-TALBOT-DARRACQ M-75

*CHASSIS 74868*

*COACHBUILDER: MILLION-GUIET*

Of the cars made under the Talbot marque, the most well-known are those created after Tony Lago purchased the company in 1935. However, between 1929 and 1934, S.T.D. was responsible for the manufacture of the M-75, a classic and memorable car designed to revitalize the Talbot name in France. A sporty creation, the M-75 had a short chassis that weighed significantly less than those of S.T.D.'s other cars, which the public had rejected for lack of speed. The model had a 2.5-liter, 6-cylinder in-line engine with a single carburetor and one overhead valve; the car was capable of speeds of up to 112 kph.

Of the approximately two hundred M-75s produced, most had basic S.T.D. factory coachwork. The custom body of Chassis 74868, however, was unique: it was created by Parisian luxury coachbuilder Million-Guiet, a company known for its deluxe work on marques such as Hispano-Suiza, Bugatti, Peugeot, and Voisin. A technique called *tout alu* ("all aluminum"), created and patented by automobile designer and stylist Jean de Vizcaya, was used to produce the car's all-aluminum alloy body. The car's coachwork was well-balanced and very much in the art deco fashion of the period, although it lacked the streamlined styling that would characterize the movement in later years. Special features included tool boxes and storage compartments built into the running boards, a fabric sunroof, and twin spare tires mounted on the rear of the trunk.

This particular M-75 has had only four owners during the course of its existence. It is believed to have been the S.T.D. show car at one of the Paris Auto Salons of the early 1930s. At some later date, a Mr. le Franc of Paris, the first known owner, acquired the M-75 from the Weismann distributor in Paris. He kept the car for a number of years before selling it to a Mr. Odenbach, who in turn sold it to race car driver Jean-Claude Fabre. Fabre had the car completely restored and from 1990 to 2007, raced it in numerous European historic car rallies. Even after participating in these events, Chassis 74868 has been driven a mere 66,000 km. Thanks to its relatively uneventful life and to the fact that it has been carefully stored out of harm's way, the M-75 remains in remarkably authentic condition. Peter Mullin purchased Chassis 74868 in 2008.

*Une* **TALBOT** *se reconnait aussi à l'élégance de sa propriétaire*

11 CV. 6 CYL. — 14/16 CV. 6 CYL. — 23 CV. 8 CYL. 1929.

R. LANG

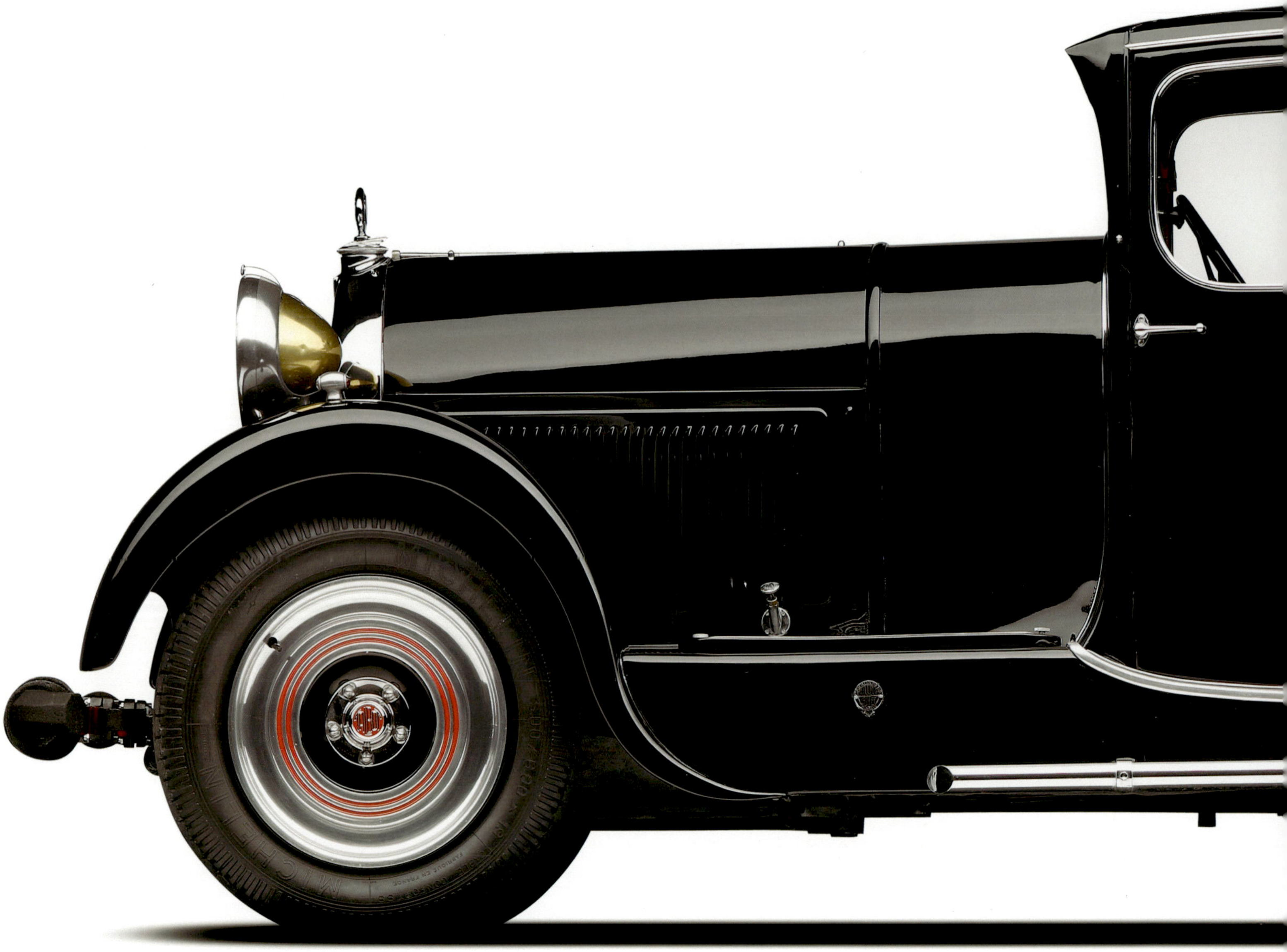

HUILE
Kilogrammes
JAEGER
8 JOURS
LICENCE K.S.
PLEIN
LITRES
ESSENCE
VIDE
S.A. VÉRITAS

*Above: Million-Guiet was a high-quality Parisian coachbuilder known for its lightweight bodies on Talbot-Lago, Delage, and Bugatti.*

*Facing page, top: It was common for Talbot-Lago to use a mix of gauge brands on the same car. Today, judges take this into consideration during their evaluations.*

*Facing page, bottom: Spark plug wires were gathered in a resin tube to keep the wiring orderly.*

TALBOT
1396-RE5

MICHELIN
F

# 1937 TALBOT-LAGO T 150-C-S

*CHASSIS 90106*

*COACHBUILDER: FIGONI & FALASCHI*

The T 150-C-S "Teardrop" was created in 1937 to publicize the reliability of Talbot-Lago and the elegance of Figoni & Falaschi coachwork. Freddy McEvoy, who was working for both companies to promote and sell cars, was reportedly drinking with American heiress Barbara Hutton in a Parisian bar when he bragged that he could drive the Teardrop from Paris to Cannes in fewer than 10 hours. He later made good on his boast, accomplishing the run in nine hours and forty-five minutes and was awarded $10,000 for the accomplishment. It was a remarkable feat of endurance before the advent of modern expressways and toll roads. The driver had to wind his way through a series of small towns and cities, along switchbacks, up and down steep grades, and over the Maritime Alps, until he finally arrived at the edge of the Mediterranean Sea. Even today, a lengthy train trip is required to make this journey. In the time before commercial air travel, the wealthy were always looking for a faster way to get from Paris to the grand hotels on the Côte d'Azur. McEvoy's exploit caught the attention of this elite group and did much to further the reputation of both Talbot-Lago and Figoni & Falaschi.

*Facing page: Translation - "To Figoni & Falaschi, the King of Coachbuilders, who has made me this remarkable sports car. Sincerely, Freddy McEvoy*
*Paris - Cannes, 9 hours 45 minutes."*

9165-RL5
à Figoni & Falaschi le Roi des
Carrossiers qui m'a fais cette
remarkable Voiture de Sport.
Sincèrement
Freddy McEvoy.
Paris – Cannes 9 heures 45 minutes.

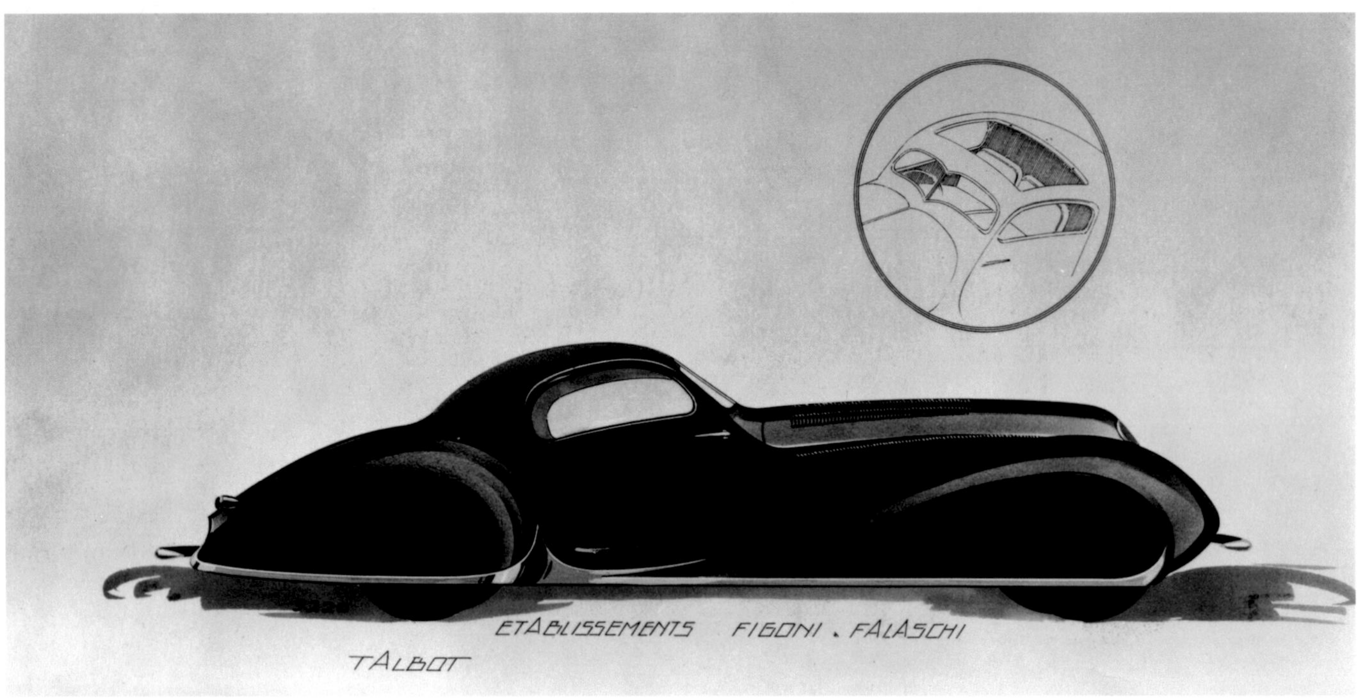


*Figoni & Falaschi styling drawings for the T 150-C-SS Teardrop in 1937.*

Teardrop, Chassis 90106, is unique in many ways: it has an aluminum alloy body, a fold-out windscreen, a sunroof, and competition-style exhaust headers. The first owner was Woolf Barnato, one of the original "Bentley boys" and chairman of Bentley Motors beginning in 1925. He saw the car when it was presented at the 1937 London Olympia Motor Show and immediately snapped it up. He sold it some time later, but it is known to have stayed in England until at least 1943, at which time a photo of it in the June 23 issue of *Motor Magazine* showed it with a new two-tone paint job.

In the early 1960s, American Otto Zipper—one of the leading importers of European automobiles on the West Coast—purchased the car. He proceeded to lend the Talbot-Lago to Briggs Cunningham's automobile museum in Costa Mesa, California, for many years. Then in 1980, the Teardrop was sold to John Calley of Beverley Hills, California, who owned it for two years before selling it to Patrick Hart of Santa Barbara, California. Hart restored the car, painted it black, and entered it in the 1984 Pebble Beach Concours d'Élégance, where it placed second in the Talbot-Lago class and also won the Moët Cup for Best French Car.

In 1985, Peter Mullin purchased the Talbot-Lago and took it to Hill and Vaughn Restorations, where it was again restored. Subsequently, Mr. Mullin has shown the Teardrop at numerous concours d'élégance throughout the world, winning many major awards. In 1990, the car was again invited to the Pebble Beach Concours d'Élégance, where it won the Gwenn Graham Trophy for Most Elegant Closed Car. The Teardrop competed at Pebble Beach again in 2000, this time winning Best in Class in the Talbot-Lago class.

*Facing page: Luigi Chinetti began his career in Paris as a race car driver and Figoni & Falaschi agent, selling Talbot-Lago T 150-C-SSs in France and its colonies.*

*Following page: In the Bois de Boulogne in Paris.*

**M. Chinetti**
**agent général** **TALBOT**

et Agent exclusif pour la France et Colonies des châssis Talbot Lago S.S. informe son aimable clientèle qu'il a fait préparer par la carrosserie

**FIGONI et FALASCHI**
**14, rue Lemoine – Boulogne-s-Seine**

plusieurs modèles hors série et particulièrement des cabriolets décapotables quatre places sur Baby quatre litres.

***LIVRABLES IMMEDIATEMENT***

De plus grâce aux accords pris avec
**TALBOT**
**et**
**FIGONI & FALASCHI**

M. Chinetti évitera à sa clientèle les délais excessivement longs pour la livraison d'une carrosserie, de modèle, ligne et couleur au choix et garantit la livraison dans les 21 jours à dater de la commande.

**M. Chinetti et C$^{ie}$**
**AGENCE** **TALBOT**
**8, r. de Pâtures (16$^{e}$) – Jasmin 15-69**
(avenue de Ver

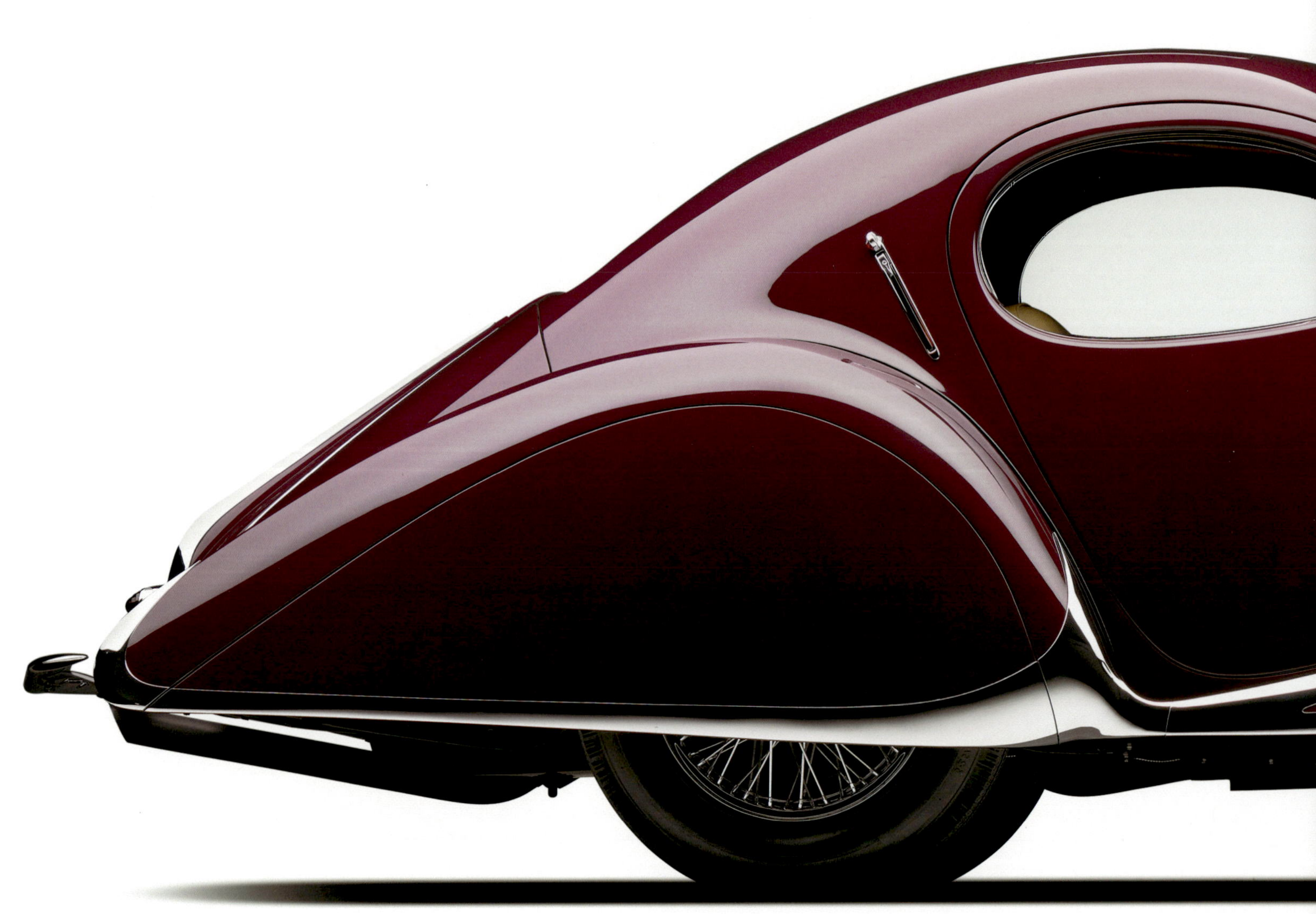

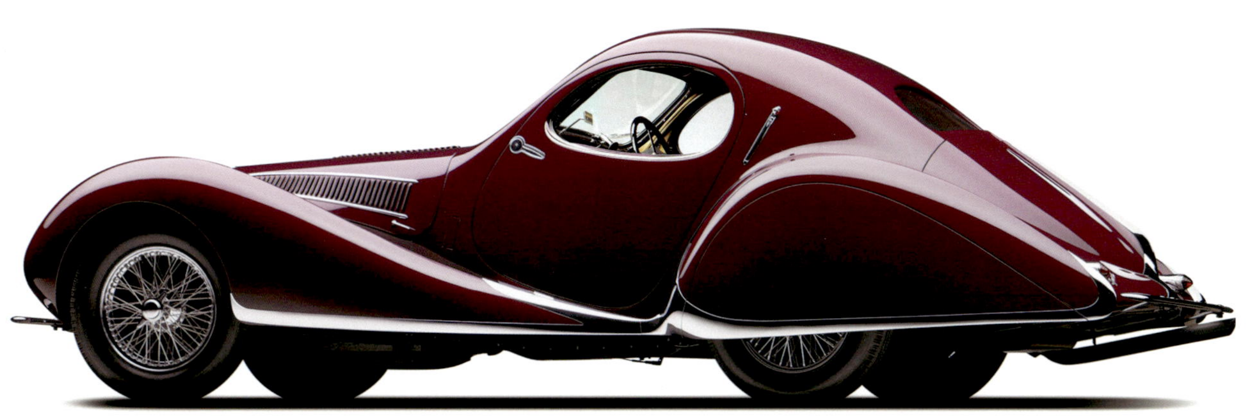

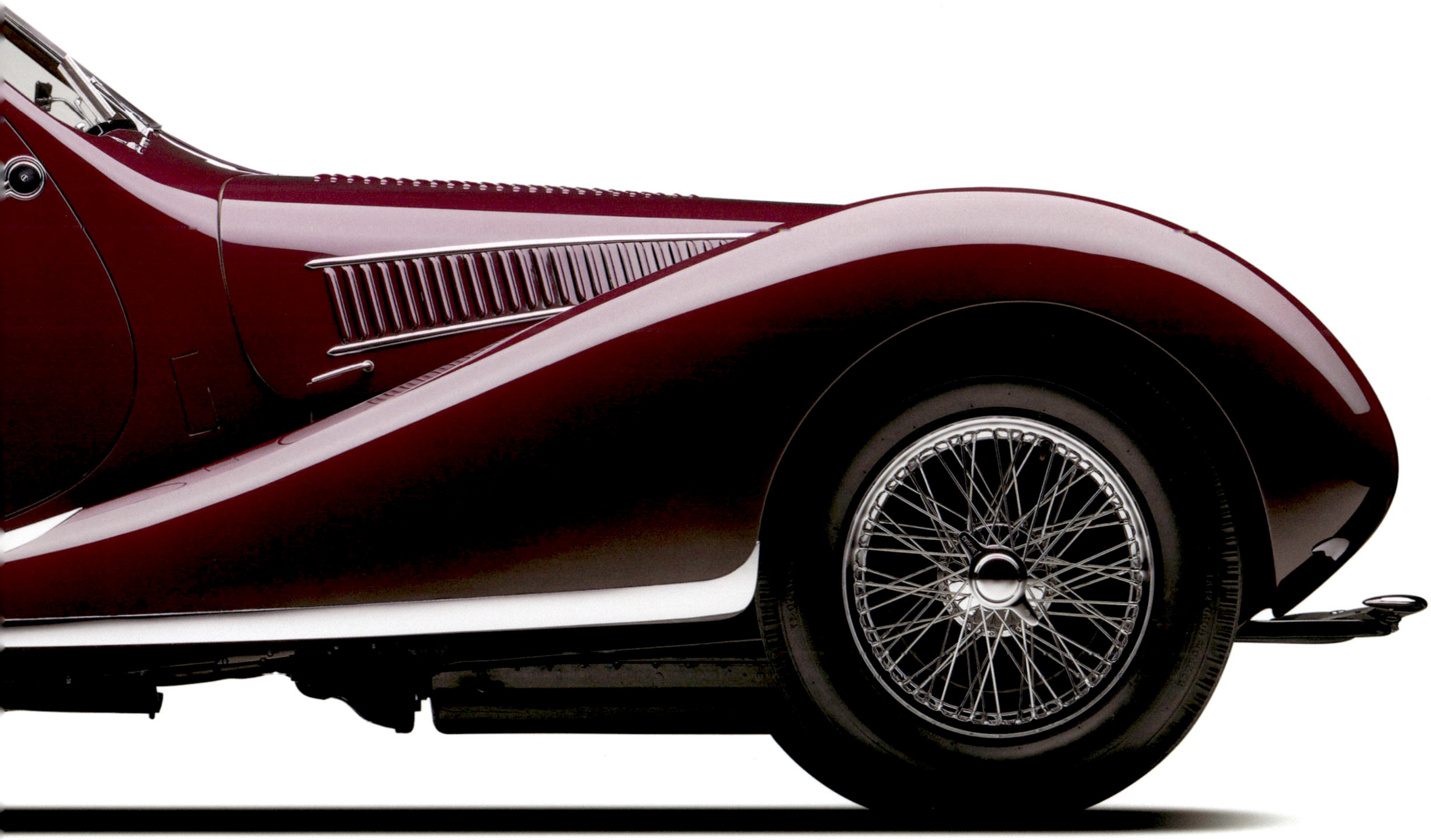

*The scalloped wood on the top of the door is a signature of Figoni's interior styling.*

Lago
Special

# 1936 TALBOT-LAGO T 26-SS

## *CHASSIS 90203*

## *COACHBUILDER: (ORIGINAL BODY) FIGONI & FALASCHI*

Everyone familiar with the world of classic cars knows that vehicles are often transformed at the whim of an owner. However, it sometimes happens that a car's metamorphosis is officially decreed by the factory: Chassis 90203 is one such vehicle.

Chassis 82930 was the first in a series of special factory race cars; as a prototype, it was updated and improved constantly throughout its competitive career. This car was delivered to Figoni & Falaschi in 1936. It was given the open race car body of a Type 150-C-SS with a short wheelbase chassis, the intent being to add the car to the Talbot-Lago racing team and to sell similarly bodied cars to private individuals. But Tony Lago was unhappy with the original work and sent the car back to Joseph Figoni for a new body. The result was a big success, and it appeared with its new styling on the Figoni & Falaschi stand at the 1937 Paris Auto Salon as one of two bodies on short wheelbase chassis. It was also displayed at the 1938 Brussels Auto Salon and the 1938 and 1939 London Motor Shows. Without exception, it was always well received.

René Dreyfus drove the car for the Talbot-Lago racing team in the 1936 season but had little success, as the factory was still ironing out the bugs. Development was complete by 1937, and new driver Raymond Sommer placed second in the Grand Prix of Pau. That same year, Gianfranco Comotti drove the car in the Marseilles Grand Prix to a second place finish, in the Grand Prix de l'ACF to a second place finish, and in the Grand Prix of Tunisie to a first place finish. However, as Talbot-Lago was still sorting out its racing program and finances were inadequate, race entries and successes were limited.

*Above: René Dreyfus with Chassis 82930, at the 3 Hours of Marseille in 1936; he did not finish the race. This car would later become Chassis 90203, a T 26-SS.*

*Facing page: René Dreyfus with his T 150-C, Chassis 82930, at the 1936 Grand Prix de l'ACF; he finished in 9th place.*

52 TALBOT

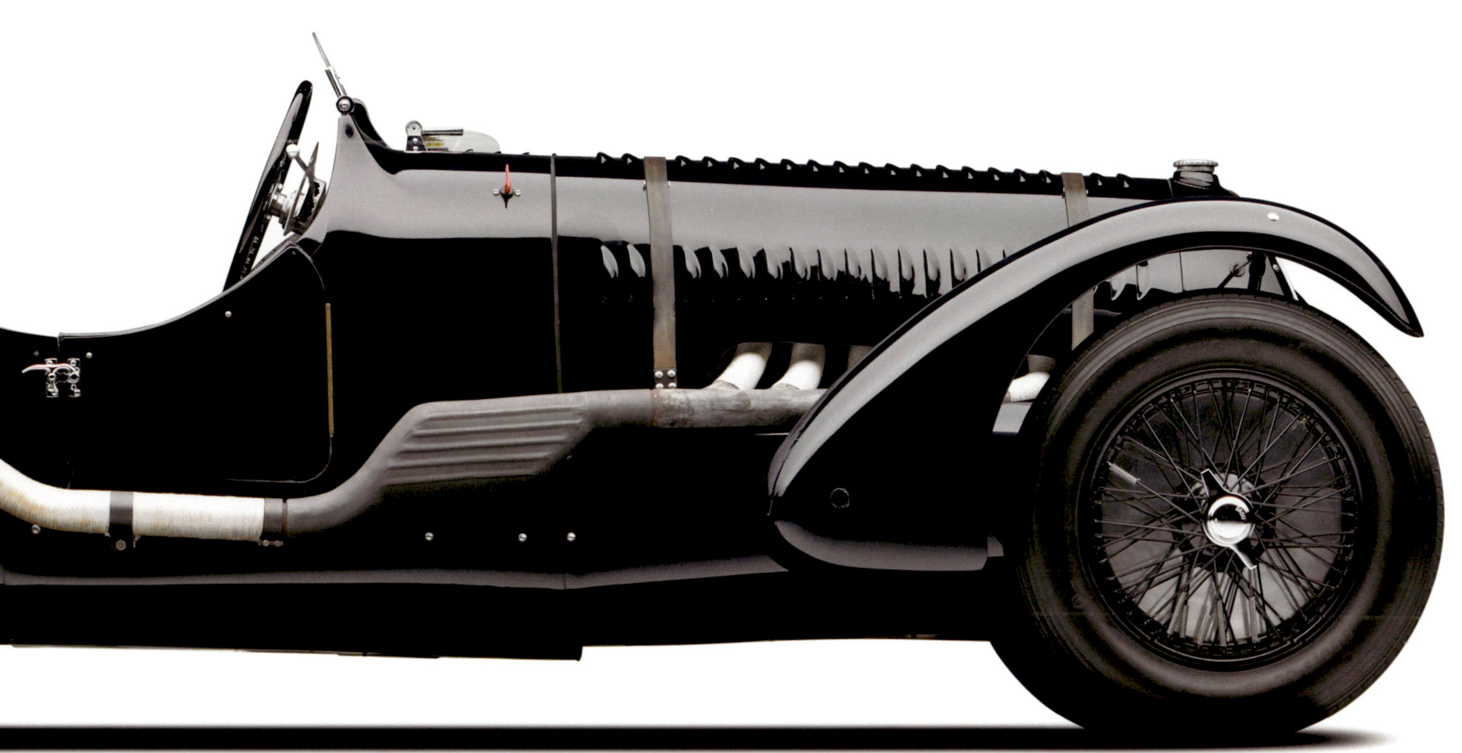

*The shift lever for the semi-automatic Wilson pre-select transmission.*

*The quick release gas cap was a French racing standard.*

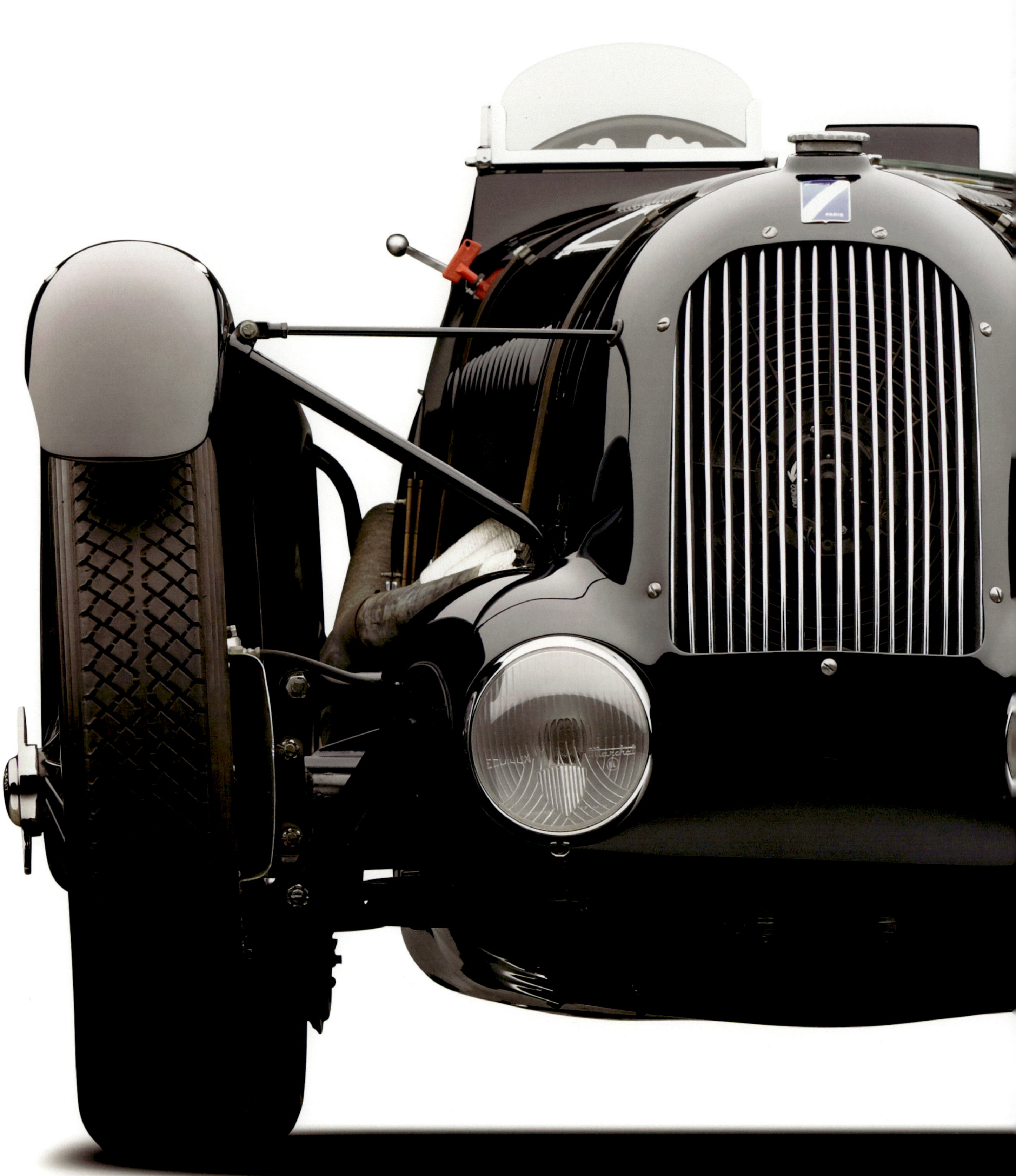

Tony Lago soon recruited Dreyfus to manage Talbot-Lago's racing team, relieving him of his duties as primary driver. Under Dreyfus's direction, the factory installed a new 4.5-liter motor (number 45003) in 1938, and the chassis was renumbered as 82933 to reflect the alteration. The car then participated in the 24 Heures de Spa-Francorchamps and the Liège-Rome-Liège rally, crashing in both races. It was repaired and continued to compete, but without any marked success. The following year, 1939, the factory again updated the chassis number, this time to 90203, to reflect a new model designation of Type 26-SS. For a manufacturer like Talbot-Lago, such chassis number changes were standard procedure when updating models and styles.

Racing team owner Luigi Chinetti purchased the car in 1939 after its final chassis number change. It was raced at Le Mans that same year but because of tire failure, it was forced to settle for second place during the forty-fifth lap. This was the car's last race prior to World War II; it was put into storage for the duration of the conflict.

In 1946, the car was sold to Charles Pozzi, who had it rebodied by Chappe Brothers, a small, local shop in France. The body was redesigned for an updated, post-war look that was more in keeping with the automotive styles of the time; unfortunately, the equally beautiful coachwork created by Joseph Figoni was destroyed. Pozzi raced the car in the 1947 season to a fifth place finish at the Circuit of Strasbourg, and Eugène Chaboud drove it to two third place finishes in the Grand Prix de l'ACF and the Grand Prix du Comminges, and to a second place finish, its best performance, at the Coupe du Salon. For the 1948 and 1949 seasons, the car participated in various French events, but it was no longer competitive, and so Pozzi retired the Type 26-SS from racing.

In 1952, Pozzi sold the car to Pierre Meyrat, who entered it in a few races with no results, then kept it for ten years before selling it to French car dealer Jacques du Montant. Jonny Thuybaert acquired the race car in 1965 and sold it to Uwe Hucke in 1976. Count Hubertus von Doenhoff purchased the car in 1992 but kept it for only a short time. He sold it to Peter Mullin that same year, who had it mechanically restored and has raced it continuously every year since in both Europe and the United States.

# 1948 TALBOT-LAGO T 26-GS

*CHASSIS 110101*

*COACHBUILDER: JACQUES SAOUTCHIK*

The Talbot-Lago Type 26 Grand Sport was first introduced at the 1947 Paris Auto Salon as a bare chassis, and was comparable in price to a top-of-the-line Delahaye, and twice the price of the single Ford model shown at the salon.

The 2.65-meter chassis of the Type 26-GS was based on two very successful pre-World War II racing models: the open Type 150-C-SS and the famous Figoni & Falaschi Teardrop Coupé, two different bodies built on the same chassis model. The Grand Sport was updated with a transverse leaf front suspension and had a 4.5-liter engine with twin aluminum overhead camshafts, three Zenith-Stromberg carburetors, and a compression ratio of 6.5:1, all of which created a car with 190 bhp and top speeds of over 200 kph. That kind of velocity grabbed the attention of spectators and media alike; in its October 1948 edition, *AutoCar* described the Type 26-GS as having "the fastest production chassis in the world... stands only chest high and is an example of striking overall lines." The Grand Sport models were successful in the endurance races of the period, such as Le Mans, and were also popular at the various concours d'élégance. Chassis 110101 participated in the 1950 Concours d'Élégance de la Place Vendôme and the 1951 Concours d'Élégance d'Enghein.

A total of thirty-six cars were produced in the Type 26-GS series, each one a custom order for a wealthy patron. Chassis 110101, originally painted in two shades of blue and boasting interior fittings in gold plate, was the very first model of the initial series. Its coachwork was created by Jacques Saoutchik, a Russian émigré who became one of France's premier coachbuilders. Although not confirmed, it is likely that this chassis was the one displayed at the 1948 Paris Auto Salon and the 1949 Brussels Auto Salon. Attendees at both events admired the Talbot-Lago on display, calling it flamboyant and original.

Initial ownership is unclear, but the trail can be picked up in Painesville, Ohio, in the early 1960s when Edsel Pfobe purchased the car from an unknown person in West Virginia. Pfobe owned the Grand Sport for a few years before selling it to Marvin Newman, who had it restored and shown at automotive events. Jacques Harguindeguy of Walnut Creek, California, purchased Chassis 110101 in 1975, had further restoration done, and finally sold it to Peter Mullin in 1989.

Réalités
SALON DE L'AUTOMOBILE 1949

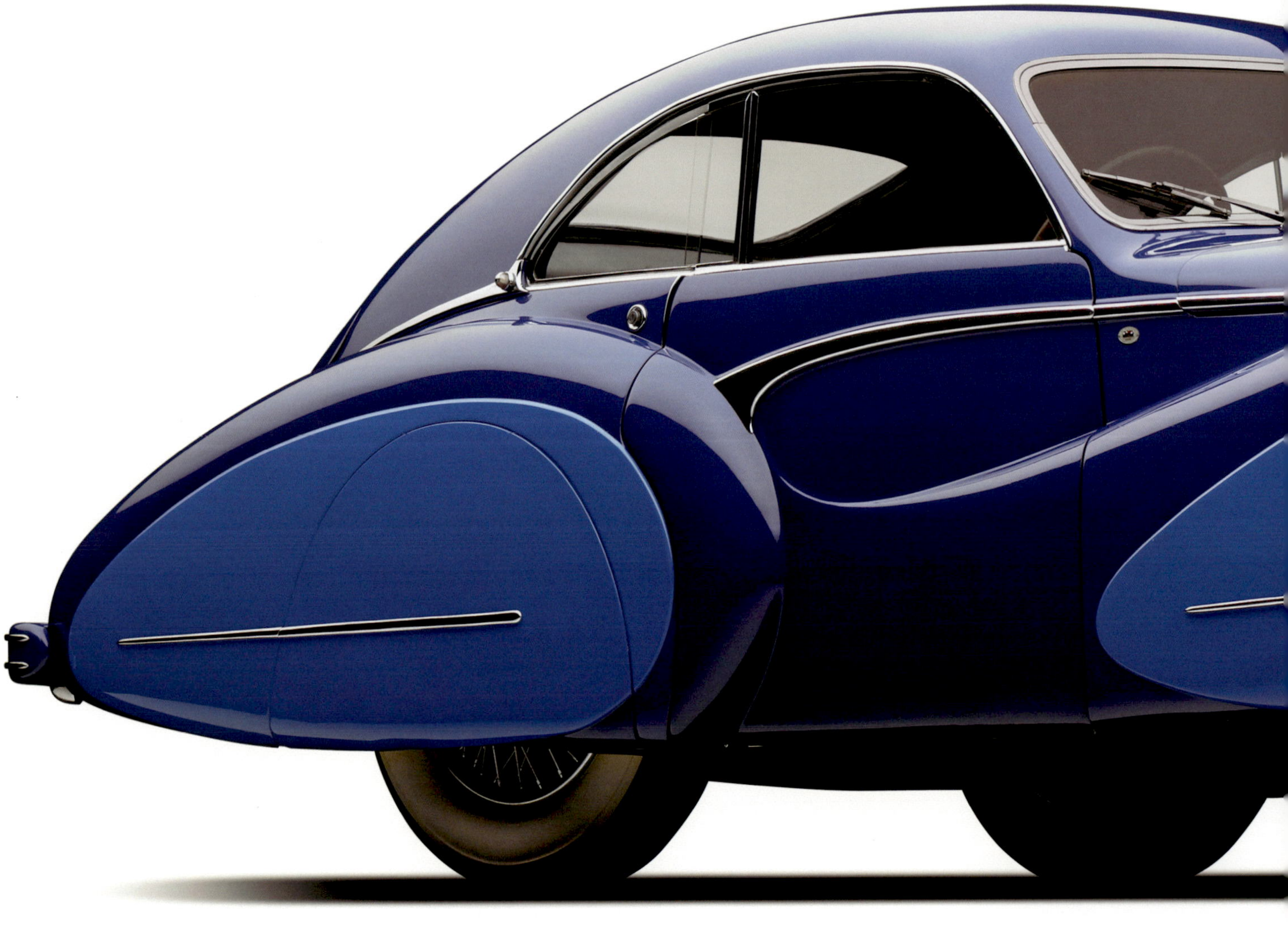

TALBOT

*The faces of the gauges are painted to match the body color. The bezels are gold plated.*

*Saoutchik put a coachbuilder plaque on the exterior of every car his company made.*

# 1950 TALBOT-LAGO T 26-GP

*CHASSIS 110052*

*COACHBUILDER:* TALBOT-LAGO FACTORY

In the late 1940s, with race cars evolving toward ever-faster speeds, European racing authorities decided to create a new competitive group for the fastest, most powerful, and most technologically advanced cars. The result was the Formula One category, founded in 1948, which established two sets of regulations, one for supercharged cars and one for unsupercharged models. The former were limited to 1.5 liter engines, while the latter were allowed motors of up to 4.5 liters.

When designing its debut entry for the Formula One category, Talbot-Lago chose to create an unsupercharged 4.5-liter car. This formula made sense for the marque. Although Talbot-Lago did operate a factory racing team, it was small and its financial resources were limited. Most of the Talbot-Lagos competing on the racing circuit were owned by private entrants, and as such they did not have mechanical support from the factory. It was therefore logical for Talbot-Lago to build sturdy, uncomplicated cars that would require minimal maintenance.

The Type 26 was produced in two series. The first set, produced from 1948 to 1950, used motors with 200 bhp at 4500 rpm, three Zenith-Stromberg carburetors, and Wilson pre-selector gear box transmissions (Chassis 110101, on page 220, is an example of these specifications). The second series, produced between 1950 and 1952, differed in the addition of a twin plug ignition, which created an additional 50 bhp. Cars from the second series were capable of a top speed of more than 267 kph.

Chassis 110052 was the second of the ten cars produced in the second series of the Type 26. It began as a factory car in 1950; that year, Talbot-Lago entered it in the various grand prix of Europe. It took forth in the Grand Prix of Belgium on June 18 and eighth in the Grand Prix de l'ACF on July 2. It also competed in Argentina's 500 Miles of Rafaela on December 24, where it was driven by South American race car driver Froilan Gonzalez, although it did not finish the race. The following year, it was sold to Octave John "Johnny" Claes, a race car driver of Belgian and British descent.

OT-LAGO

LF50

LF50

LR-50

Claes entered his new Type 26 in all the major European races of 1951, including the Grand Prix of Switzerland, Belgium, Holland, Germany, San Rémo, Spain, and Turin. Unfortunately, the car's contemporary racing career came to a screeching halt in 1952. That year, Claes agreed to lend the car to his friend, noted Belgian driver André Pilette, who intended to race it in the Grand Prix d'Albi. Claes however, didn't get the car to his friend until the night before the race; Pilette had no time to practice and as a result, he was gridded in last place. Then halfway through the first lap, the gas cap flew off and Pilette was soaked in fuel. He immediately went to the pit, where he changed his shirt while the crew fixed the car. Pilette returned to the race, but his concentration was ruined and he crashed in the tenth lap, breaking his leg. The car, which was damaged severely, was impounded for investigation by the authorities, who proceeded to store the Type 26 on a dock at the Port of Anvers in Antwerp. Exposed to the elements, uncovered and unattended, theft and deterioration meant that the car was soon missing a number of parts.

Paul Swaelens, a high-profile French race car driver, acquired the car from Claes in 1953 and even managed to recover some of the missing parts and pieces; but because it was no longer competitive on the racing circuit, he did not do much with it. Car dealer Anthony "Tony" Mottram bought Chassis 110052 in 1974 and began refurbishing it, although he did not complete the process. Four years later, the car was purchased by Count Hubertus von Doenhoff, who sent it to Paul Grist's shop in England to finish the restoration. The Count also sent Grist another Type 26, Chassis 110004. This car was from the first Type 26 production series and had the less potent single plug ignition, but von Doenhoff wanted it restored for optimal competitiveness. At the Count's request, the engines from the two cars were switched and the more powerful version was placed in Chassis 110004. The cars were then returned to the Count, who used both Type 26s in vintage racing events.

Von Doenhoff sold Chassis 110052 in 1986 to Colin Crabbe, an English dealer and former race car driver, who in 1991 sold it at auction to Swiss collector Eric Traber. Peter Mullin acquired the car shortly after in 1992. He then later purchased Chassis 110004, which still had Chassis 110052's motor that Paul Grist had switched out several years earlier. In the spirit of stewardship, Mr. Mullin restored both motors to their original chassis and configurations. Mr. Mullin currently races Chassis 110052 in vintage events.

*The chassis plates were riveted in place to prevent racing teams from switching them. Teams sometimes used this tactic to save money on import duties.*

# 1951 TALBOT-LAGO T 26-GS

*CHASSIS 110160*

*COACHBUILDER: STABILIMENTI FARINA*

The technical specifications of Chassis 110160 are identical to those of Talbot-Lago Grand Sport Chassis 110101; for a review of those details, please refer to page 220.

In 1950, a Portuguese car collector with a partiality for Talbot-Lagos ordered a Grand Sport chassis from the factory in Paris. He talked to several coachbuilders in France, but settled on a design by Italy's Stabilimenti Farina for a two-passenger drophead coupé. He therefore sent the chassis to Turin, Italy, in late 1950 with instructions to complete the car in time for the 1951 Paris Auto Salon. The owner was very involved with the coachbuilding process; he visited Stabilimenti Farina twice and had the car's hood lowered and several other minor modifications made to suit his taste. He took delivery of the car at the Paris Auto Salon, and then drove back to Turin to settle the bill. The owner then insisted that the wooden mock-up used to design the car be destroyed so no one else could have a Talbot-Lago like his. Chassis 110160 was the only Italian body ever commissioned on a Talbot-Lago; such chassis were usually the province of Figoni & Falaschi, Jacques Saoutchik, and other French luxury coachbuilders.

This Grand Sport was featured in the December 1951 issue of *Road and Track* magazine, which covered the Paris Auto Salon of that year. The glowing review celebrated the car's "full complement of useful, as well as luxurious equipment" and noted the Italian coachbuilder's use of "a fluted chrome strip along the front fender and the heavy bar of chrome across the top of the strictly Italian grille," all of which were a nod to French taste.

The owner of Chassis 110160 took his prize back to Portugal, where Jacques Touzet, another car enthusiast, fell in love with it the moment it arrived in Lisbon. Touzet followed the owner around for two years, contacting him repeatedly regarding the Grand Sport. Persistence eventually paid off when Touzet was able to buy the car in 1953. He thoroughly enjoyed his purchase for the next forty-seven years, but in 2000, he finally decided he was getting a little old for his toy. Chassis 110160 was purchased by Charles Morse, who then sold it to Peter Mullin in 2001. The car was restored from the ground up in California and entered in the 2010 Pebble Beach Concours d'Élégance, where it won First in Class.

FARINA
C.so TORTONA 12
TORINO

156 S 75

156 S 75

*The dashboard is leather covered to make it more elegant. Instrumentation is racing style.*

*The engine is a 4.5-liter twin mid-camshaft model with three carburetors.*

# 1951 TALBOT-LAGO T 15 LB

*CHASSIS 121587*

*COACHBUILDER: HENRI CHAPRON*

The Talbot-Lago Type 15 LB was a continuation of the Type 15, which had been introduced in 1936 and produced until the factory closed in 1939 because of World War II. When the factory reopened, it still had chassis for the Type 15 and continued to take orders, but sales for this older model were slow, even with new coachwork. Priced at 1,500,000 French francs, it cost more than the all-new Delahaye Type 235 and was too expensive for the post-war economic climate.

The Type 15 LB was introduced in 1951 at the Paris Auto Salon. It was offered with either a new 4- or 6-cylinder engine. Chassis 121587 has a 2.69-liter, 4-cylinder in-line motor with two carburetors and overhead valves. The car was custom bodied by Chapron and styled by Carlo Delaisse, who worked for Chapron and was well regarded for his efforts with Delage and Talbot-Lago. The car was ordered as a four-passenger, two-door coupé—a clean, modern design for the early 1950s. The Type 15 LB still has its original maroon paint and red leather interior and is remarkably complete.

The challenge for Talbot-Lago with this new model was the coachwork, which was heavy and very expensive, so much so that it affected the performance of the car's 4-cylinder motor. The result was a car that didn't sell well.

Chassis 121587 was part of the Schulmpf Reserve Collection and was stored with the rest of the cars that were involved in that legal dispute. It was locked away for forty years until purchased by Peter Mullin in 2009.

*Top: Henri Chapron badge on the front flank of the car.*
*Middle: Serial number plate inside the engine compartment.*
*Bottom: Pronounced stamping on 4-cylinder valve cover.*

3417·A

# SUGGESTED READING


Abeillon, Pierre. *Talbot-Lago de Course*. Vandoeuveres, Suisse. Paris, France. 1992

Adatto, Richard. *From Passion to Perfection—The Story of French Streamlined Styling, 1930 - 1939*. Paris, France. 2003

Adatto, Richard S. and Meredith, Diana E. *Delage Styling and Design*. Deerfield, Illinois. 2005

Adatto, Richard S. and Meredith, Diana E. *Delahaye-Styling and Design*. Philadelphia, Pennsylvania. 2006

Bellu, René. *Toutes les Voitures Françaises 1937 – Salon 1936*. Paris, France. 1997

Cabart, D., Rouxel, C. & Burgess-Wise, D. *Delage. France's Finest Car*. Deerfield, Illinois. 2008

Cohin, Edmond. *Historique de la Course Automobile 1881-1977*. Paris, France. 1966

Darmendrail, Pierre. *Le Grand Prix de Pau*. Paris, France. 1992

Dorizon, J., Peigney, F. & Dauliac, J.P. *Delahaye: Le Grand Livre*. Paris, France. 1995

Dreyfus, René with Kimes, Beverly Rae. *My Two Lives: Race Driver to Restaurateur*. Tucson, Arizona. 1983

Furman, Michael. *Motorcars of the Classic Era*. Philadelphia, Pennsylvania. 2003

Georgano, Nick (ed). *The Beaulieu Encyclopaedia of the Automobile, Volume I, A-L*. United Kingdom. 2000

Georgano, Nick (ed). *The Beaulieu Encyclopaedia of the Automobile, Volume I, M-Z*. United Kingdom. 2000

Georgano, Nick. *The Beaulieu Encyclopedia of the Automobile: Coachbuilding*. United Kingdom. 2001

Lamm, Michael and Holls, David. *A Century of Automotive Style*. Stockton, California. 1996

Merksamer, Gregg D. *A History of the New York International Auto Show 1900–2000*. Atlanta, Georgia. 2000

Moity, C., Teissedre, J.M. & Bienvenu, A. *24 Heures du Mans 1923-1992*. Paris, France. 1992

Prince Birabongse. *Bits and Pieces: Being Motor Racing Collections of B Bira*. London, England. 1947

Simeone, Dr. Frederick A. *The Spirit of Competition*. Philadelphia, Pennsylvania. 2009

Spitz, Alain. *Talbot, des Talbot-Darracq aux Talbot-Lago (Prestige de l'automobile)*. Paris, France. 1983

Stein, Jonathan A. *Curves of Steel: Streamlined Automobile Design*. Philadelphia, Pennsylvania. 2007

Šuman-Hreblay, Marián. *Dictionary of World Coachbuilders and Car Stylists*. Liptovský Mikuláš, Slovakia. 2003

Tissot, Jean-Paul. *Delahaye: La Belle Carrosserie Française*. Paris, France. 2006

# ACKNOWLEDGEMENTS/IMAGE CREDITS

Our warmest thanks go to the many friends and colleagues who have given us the benefit of their knowledge, provided images from their private archives, and taken the time to read and fact-check the material collected in this book.

We are grateful to Claude Figoni, for giving us new information and photos from his family archives; Daniel Cabart, for fact-checking the Delage section and providing images not previously published; Noelle Chapron, for assisting with photos and original documents; Jean-Pierre Bernard, for his contributions as past president of the Delahaye Club and Delahaye factory sales manager; Dr. Fred Simeone and the Simeone Automotive Museum Archive for providing rare images and documents; The Philadelphia Free Library; Jean-Paul Tissot, president of the Delahaye Club, for giving us images from his private archives; Diana Meredith, for reviewing the manuscript and allowing us to use material published in our prior books; William E. Connor II, Malcolm Pray, J. Willard Marriott, Jr., and John W. Rich for the comparative presentation of their cars; Susan Bendrick, for her coordination of the Mullin Automotive Museum team; Caroline Alley, Greg Delfs, Jessica Delfs, Jim Dowd, Webb Farrer, Kathleen McCafferty, Andrew Reilly, and Ruby Talbot; and Sandra Button, chairwoman of the Pebble Beach Concours d'Élégance, for supporting our efforts.

Further appreciation goes to David Phillips, Senior Artist at Michael Furman Studio for helping create the modern photographs that fill this book; Mary Dunham, Senior Designer at Michael Furman Studio for giving the book its form; Phil Neff, for his thoughtful project management and image identification; photographic assistants Esteban Granados, David March, Dan Mezick, and Jim Mital; Bob Tursack and his staff at Brilliant Graphics for once again providing beautiful printing that has brought all of our efforts to life.

This book would not have been possible without you.

## IMAGE CREDITS

All modern studio photography by Michael Furman.

Historic photographs, documents and printed matter courtesy of the following:
Adatto Archives
Daniel Cabart
Noelle Chapron
Claude Figoni
Mullin Automotive Museum Archives
Phil Neff
Julien Philippy
Simeone Foundation Automotive Museum Archives
Jean-Paul Tissot

# COLOPHON

Mullin Automotive Museum
1421 Emerson Avenue
Oxnard, CA 93033
www.MullinAutomotiveMuseum.com

*French Curves: Delahaye • Delage • Talbot-Lago*
*Mullin Automotive Museum*
published by:
Coachbuilt Press
Philadelphia, Pennsylvania, USA
www.CoachbuiltPress.com

*French Curves: Delahaye • Delage • Talbot-Lago*
*Mullin Automotive Museum*

First Edition August, 2011

ISBN 9780977980994
Library of Congress Control Number: 2011911958

Creative Director: Michael Furman
Design by: Mary Dunham
Digital Art: David Phillips
Project Coordinator: Phil Neff
Printed by: Brilliant Graphics, Exton, Pennsylvania, USA
Press: Heidelberg XL105 Speedmaster
Screening: 400 lpi Heidelberg Hybrid
Paper: Sappi Galerie Art Gloss, 100# Text
Inks: Toyo Process & PMS 426 with carbon black for the duotones
Bindery: Bindery Associates, Lancaster, Pennsylvania, USA
Fonts: Futura; Bold, Light, Light Oblique
MostraOne; Bold, Regular
MostraTwo; Bold
Neutraface Text; Light Italic